PARENTING FROM PRISON

PARENTING FROM PRISON

A Hands-on Guide for
Incarcerated Parents

James M. Birney

Algonquin, IL
2011

Copyright © 2011 by James M. Birney
All rights reserved under International and Pan-American
Copyright Conventions.

ISBN 978-1460992326

No part of this book may be reproduced or transmitted in any form or by any means, electronic or mechanical-including photocopying, recording, or by any information storage and retrieval system-without permission in writing from the publisher.

To God,
who deserves all glory

Contents

Introduction..ix
1. A Child's Development Needs...1
2. Preparing to Parent from Prison 31
3. What a Child Asks...50
4. Visiting with Your Child..69
5. Activities to Stay Connected..96

Introduction

It is estimated that 2,000,000 children in the United States have a parent behind bars. If you are reading this book, you're most likely one of the parents of these children or you know someone who is, and it is your desire to reach out and help them with the additional emotional burdens they are facing.

Unfortunately, there are relatively few programs or agencies focused on helping an incarcerated parent build and maintain a healthy and positive relationship with their child. This book was written for the parent in prison who is seeking to establish or grow a quality relationship with their child.

Each child's emotional situation is unique, as well the circumstances surrounding your incarceration, and the home environment your child is now in. As such, it is extremely important to remember that your child's best interests are the main goal and priority in determining the appropriate parenting strategy to employ. If there is any question about how to proceed, please seek the advice of a professional therapist or counselor. This book was written for those situations where establishing and growing a relationship is in your child's best interest.

Parenting any child is typically a big challenge. Parenting a child, when you are an incarcerated parent, can seem overwhelming but it is not impossible. It is a unique experience that requires you to adapt, your traditional parental roles and responsibilities, to the prison environment and the limitations that come with it.

As a child develops and grows, they are faced with learning a wide range of new physical and emotional skills. The separation of a parent, due to an incarceration, often creates a situation where the child is unable to progress along the typical emotional development path. This disruption generally occurs because the child is exposed to new, additional or more powerful feelings, which have the overall effect of weakening their ability to cope and normally progress emotionally.

The range of feelings a child may experience can be very broad. They can include anger, rage, abandonment, rejection, hopelessness, powerlessness, loss, sadness, fear, guilt, disbelief, anxiety and confusion. It is important to help children understand and work through their feelings. There is only one way or you to do this with your child - to stay connected to them in a healthy, positive and supportive way.

A healthy connection (relationship attachment to you) with your child is based on a strong foundation of love and trust and is maintained through consistent parenting. Trust and attachment is

Introduction

critical for a child's development and is more fully discussed in Chapter 1 – A Child's Development Needs.

Consistent parenting allows a child to develop trust in you, that you are going to be there for them over the long haul, that they can share their feelings with you, that you will be there to encourage them and that you'll continually guide and support them. Chapter 2 - Preparing to Parent From Prison, details many of the steps required to prepare yourself for parenting your child and includes a sample Parenting Plan.

A child typically asks lots of questions. Your child will ask even more questions. They need honest answers to build trust with you and to more completely understand the situation and feelings they are now experiencing. Chapter 3 – What a Child Asks, identifies and answers the four key questions they will ask you. In addition, this chapter also looks at two critical questions they want to ask you but typically don't.

Despite the challenges and potential issues, personal visits can be one of the most effective ways to connect to your child. Preparing yourself, your child and their caregiver are essential to a successful visit and are reviewed more fully in Chapter 4 – Visiting with Your Child.

Every contact you have with your child is an opportunity to strengthen your relationship and become more connected to them. Activities, separate from visits and phone calls, are a powerful strategy to increase your interaction with your child and become more actively involved in their life. Chapter 5 - Activities to Stay

INTRODUCTION

Connected, presents over thirty activities that will get you more involved with your child.

You can have a strong connection to your child, even despite the challenges you are facing with being incarcerated. Providing your child with love, emotional support, and encouragement are of critical importance to them and will also bring you a renewed sense of hope and strength.

- 1 -

A Child's Development Needs

Parenting plays a critical part in a child's overall development. A child's overall development encompasses a wide range of physical, intellectual, social, emotional and moral development processes. Your role as a parent is to facilitate these processes while providing for your child with the overall love, care, nurturing and protection they need.

When children are dealing with a trauma, such as having a parent in prison, it diverts their emotional energy and moves them away from their required development processes. It is especially important to remember that children are always traumatized by any parental separation. It has a very profound effect on them and can lead to trust issues and behavioral problems.

A child suffering separation trauma, related to a parental incarceration, has unique features. This type of child typically experiences feelings of shame, guilt and low self-esteem. These feelings can impact a child developmentally, especially in the areas of areas of intellectual progression, social development, emotional maturity and moral development.

Child development is obviously a very broad topic and much has been written on the subject. However, for the purpose of reviewing the potential impact to a child, that may arise from a parent's incarceration, our focus will be concentrated on the following key child development areas.

Physical development: this development area involves changes in physical maturity of the body including its size, shape, coordination and other physical abilities.

Intellectual development: this area involves the learning and use of language, a child's ability to problem solve, the ability to reason, the ability to organize thoughts and ideas, and is generally related to the intellectual growth of the brain.

Social development: this development area involves the process of gaining the skills and knowledge necessary to interact successfully with other people, including parents, family and friends.

Emotional development: this child development area deals with a child's feelings and emotions particularly involving a child's response to events. It involves the development of a child's understanding of their own feelings and appropriate ways of expressing those feelings.

Moral and Spiritual development: this area of development involves a child's basic understanding of right and wrong, in addition to the changes in behavior that arise from that understanding. A child develops a conscience during this stage of development. Spiritual development involves a child's relationship to God and the religious practices of the family.

A child's development in these five key areas is obviously impacted by many factors, but the absence of a parent or caregiver primarily impacts their parental attachment; a fundamental factor in child development. Through this attachment, a parent is able to guide the child in each of the above development areas. In addition to providing overall guidance, parents with strong attachment to their children can provide encouragement during tough times, teach them coping skills and support deeper family relationships that the child will be able to rely on during challenging periods in their development.

A child's basic needs can be grouped into three primary areas: developmental, attachment and depth of relationships. A child's developmental, attachment and depth of relationships (D.A.D. for short) needs, and the objectives for each of theses areas, will be reviewed over the balance of this chapter.

The D.A.D. approach will assist you in obtaining a better understanding of where your child is at currently and what needs they may now have. In the area of child development, age specific traits, goals and potential issues will be explored. In the area of attachment, a child's basic attachment needs will be reviewed along with strategies that will assist an incarcerated parent in meeting these needs. In the area of depth of relationships, strategies will be reviewed for expanding your child's care-giving support structure, in order to provide them with a network that will help them through the separation trauma.

The table on the following page summarizes the basic development phases of children and provides a summary of the traits, goals and potential issues for each of the described age segments.

Developmental Phases, Traits Goals & Potential Issues

Phases	Traits	Goals	Potential Issues
Infants Age 0 - 2	Total Dependence	Trust Attachment	Lack of Bonding, Non-Parent Dependency
Early Childhood Age 3 - 6	Increased Understanding, Awareness of Self, Mobility	Sense of Power, Independence, Initiative	Trust & Attachment, Stress, Anxiety, Regression, Slow dev.
Middle Childhood Age 7 - 10	Some Independence, Basic Reasoning, Peer Influence	Owning Actions & Emotions, Work Ethic, Productiveness	Trust & Attachment, Distancing Oneself, Shame, Acting Out,
Late Childhood Age 11 - 13	Basic Goal Setting, Forward Thinking, Motivated Behavior, Puberty	Self-Aware, Self Motivated, Group Productiveness, Emotional Control	Trust Issues, Anti-Social, Rebellion, Stress, Breaking Rules & Limits
Teen/ Young Adult Age 14 - 18	Independence, Future Thinking, Emotional Turmoil, Sexual Development	Life-Aware, Conflict Resolution, Identity, Work and Relationships	Aggression, Withdrawal, Rejection of Parent, Rebellion, Crime

It's important to remember that the above summary and the following descriptions make general statements about when development occurs in a child's life. Each child will nevertheless develop at his or her own speed and that even within a particular development phase certain traits may progress faster than others. In addition, having a parent in prison poses a unique set of challenges, for each child, during each particular phase of development.

For infants: during the first year or two of your child's life, it may not seem to you that your child would react to your incarceration, but this is an extremely important phase of a child's development. Infants are learning the basics of connecting or attaching to their parents and or caregivers. This is a time when they are learning to trust in adults, that the adult will be there to meet their needs. In this development stage, infants may definitely sense the absence of a parent. They may even miss a parent that was consistently available to them prior to their incarceration. If a primary parent is now no longer present, due to going to prison, it may seriously impact the development of trust and attachment with this child.

Infants may develop new attachments, to alternative caregivers, during this time. However, their basic attachment and trust developments goals may be threatened by: removal of one parent, placement in another home, multiple caregivers or a general disruption in parenting routines.

For early childhood: children begin testing their attachments, with parents or other primary caregivers, to see if these bonds will support them as they explore new needs in their life. During this phase, they are developing a sense of independence, initiative and power. Exercising these traits will often lead them to start taking small steps to test their attachments to you, such as seeing your reaction when they defy you, when they say no to you or when they run away from a troubling or difficult situation.

A child's exercising of their new found independence will often cause adults to react in ways that will make these children feel controlled. During this stage of development, children want to exercise independence, not be controlled, however they also want to feel safe and that you will be there for them no matter what.

The struggle of achieving baby steps of independence and becoming more aware of themselves, while still wanting to be strongly attached and loved by their caregivers, makes this development phase particularly difficult for children who are separated from a parent.

For children with a parent in prison, the early childhood phase is more difficult and their behavior reflects this difficulty. They have an internal conflict: they want to step out and learn more about themselves but they also want to have strong connections to rely on during this time. Since the connections are weakened by the absence of a parent, they often act out through negative behaviors. Tantrums and acting out are characteristics of the emotional struggles that may be seen during this stage of development.

Non-incarcerated parents or other caregivers, of children in this situation, are challenged to provide the physical and emotional support that is needed by the children going through these issues. Not only are the young children struggling to develop the appropriate traits but they are also confronted with a parent or caregiver who is struggling to cope with them and the rest of their life situation.

For middle childhood: children in this phase typically begin to exercise additional opposition, power and control. This arises from their basic emotional growth, additional reasoning skills, and strong influences from their peers. During this stage of development, they are trying to prove to themselves that they are unique and separate - that they have an identity which is distinct from their parent or primary caregiver.

During this development stage there is generally a distancing of the child from their parent or caregiver. Their thought process during this stage can be summarized as follows: "If I agree with you, I am just like you." "Since I am me, and not you, I will not agree with you." "If you make me agree with you, I will hate you and rebel against you and wish you were not here."

This approach is obviously not a well thought out and reasoned process but more of a natural instinct for a child in the early phase of middle childhood. Much of this influence may also be coming from their peers, who they see more like themselves, than they see themselves being like their parents.

Children with a parent in prison, during this stage of development, may illogically believe that they are in some way responsible for their parent's incarceration. They may be mad at their parents and subsequently "wish their parent was not around."

This thought process leads them to believe that they had a role in their parent leaving. This belief confuses their emotions and logic and may lead to behavioral issues, including sleeplessness, eating disorders, fears, nightmares, bed-wetting and acting out.

Children in this age group need to know that they have some influence on adults to help get their needs met. The importance of maintaining a connection, to an incarcerated parent, is most critical at this phase of development in order that the child avoid feelings of guilt, powerlessness, loss of control and detachment. Issues, such as these, during this development phase may have lasting consequences.

Late childhood: children are beginning to replace their parents as the center of their universe and they are becoming more self-aware, self motivated and are learning new skills. Their behavior should be motivated by forward thinking and goal setting. Children in this group are largely focused on and motivated by their peer group.

Children in this development phase probably fully understand the concept of crime and punishment. Having an incarcerated parent generally leads them to experience sadness at the detachment. It also creates a stigma with their friends, as they have a very close association with their peer group during this development stage.

Children in this group are potentially vulnerable to taunting, from their friends and they may experience feelings of embarrassment, if they are not able to fully articulate their feelings or tell the full story behind a parent's incarceration. Children need to be able to effectively communicate what's going on with them to their peers and even to adults. They need to develop a sense of competence in dealing with others and with being able to explain their family situation. Children that don't achieve these things are likely to stop talking (especially when they are away from home), avoid school, develop physical ailments and not participate in social or sporting activities.

For teenage: children much of their focus is on their identity, social status, relationships and future planning. They are continuing to strive to learn more about their own feelings, their peer's feelings and the feelings of their family members. They also are seeking to understand more fully the meaning behind people's behaviors, both positive and negative. Some children in this group struggle to understand how "right and wrong" can vary so greatly from one family to another.

Parents and caregivers of teenage children need to help them to understand their feelings without being a judge of their feelings. They need to provide their children with good role models in and outside the home. They also need to work with their children to teach them communication skills that will enable them to say what they mean and to enable them to listen with compassion and empathy.

Teenagers need to be making their own choices about how they spend their time, what activities they're doing and what friends they have. Their opinions, ideas and personal tastes should be respected. They should also have a fully developed understanding of rules and consequences.

A parent or caregiver to a teenager, with an incarcerated parent, must be genuine and honest. Adults who don't tell the truth, lie about a situation or fail to honestly express their feelings may confuse the development process of a teenager. The sending of mixed messages, telling your child one thing, but doing another, may lead to teenage behaviors that are founded on confusion and not on honesty.

Behavioral issues, in this development stage, may include increasingly aggressive behavior, inconsistency, and exaggerated reactions to limits or controls. Anger, rebellion and misbehavior (including illegal activity) may also be displayed as they reach out to solicit attention.

On the other end of the spectrum, some teenagers may display guarded, quiet, shy or closed off behaviors around adults. They have probably developed basic trust and attachment issues and have only received inconsistent attachment from their parents or caregivers. They may be "lost" in terms of achieving the development goals for this stage.

Teenagers are increasingly out in the real world, attempting to figure out who they really are, where they're going and who they want to have ongoing relationships with. They are making value judgments and generally taking more risks. A certain level of risk-taking is normal however, their risk taking may be increased because they may have been raised in a generally more disruptive, chaotic or risk oriented environment.

Their environment may have exposed them to drugs, financial problems, domestic abuse, parental stress or any other number of stressful or traumatic situations. These can impact their attempt to figure out who they really are and where they are going, as their sense of what a normal lifestyle should be is not what is generally considered normal.

Many teenagers have been forced to assume an adult role at a very early age. Some have been left alone excessively, or left as a caregiver, for long periods of time without supervision. Children in this situation may react in a variety of ways. For some, they fear that they will follow in their incarcerated parent's footsteps, creating a lingering anxiety that can become overpowering and prevent them from normal development. Other teenagers may develop a sense of rejection, originating from their incarcerated parent, or develop anger towards them for putting them in the situation they are currently in.

It is difficult to determine how a teenager will react developmentally and it depends largely upon their age, family circumstances, home environment, parental stress, parental care, nature of their parent's crime and the surrounding support network that they may have.

All of these factors can contribute to an emotional crisis for some teenagers. In these situations, it is difficult to determine the full and specific impact of the parent's incarceration. Despite the uniqueness of each individual situation, teenagers in general have a very strong need for honesty, consistency and stability in their lives. Teenagers, especially boys, need supportive adult role models who can provide adult interaction and the affection that may be missing from their lives due to their parent's incarceration.

Separation from a parent, who is incarcerated, will generate any number of feelings and will definitely impact a child during each of the development phases. Generally, the separation creates feelings similar to those that someone would feel at the death of a loved one, including:

- Shock and denial - the child reacts very little and may even refuse to believe what has really happened or they may even give the appearance of accepting what has happened.
- Anger and protest - these rebellious feelings can dominate a child while the parent is away.
- Despair - the child may feel helpless as they may not fully understand or be not able to change the situation. It also can lead to depression, withdrawal or even guilt for what has happened.
- Acceptance - the child begins to accept the fact that the incarcerated parent is not returning home soon and begins to behave and develop more normally again.

Attachment:

Children require attachment to parents or caregivers so that they may develop self-reliance and an ability to trust others, a big factor in all child development stages. A child's ability to be attached to their parents, or other significant caregivers, is the primary means by which they trust others, develop a conscience, learn to get along with others, and develop positive self-esteem. Attachment is one of the most basic tasks in child development.

Attachment to a family unit is essential for giving children a sense of their cultural identity and for belonging to a family that shares certain values and beliefs. Cultural identity includes a family's values, belief system, religious beliefs, a manner of dress, manner of speaking, communication and standards of behaving. This cultural or family identity promotes positive feelings of self-esteem in children and assists them during each development phase.

Attachment generally occurs via a process where a child feels a discomfort or a need and expresses that need to their parent or caregiver. When the parent or caregiver meets that need, the child is comforted and an attachment is developed or strengthened. This process occurs continually during each development phase from infancy through teenage years. It is this attachment that provides an emotional anchor for children to rely on during their development.

Child Attachment Process

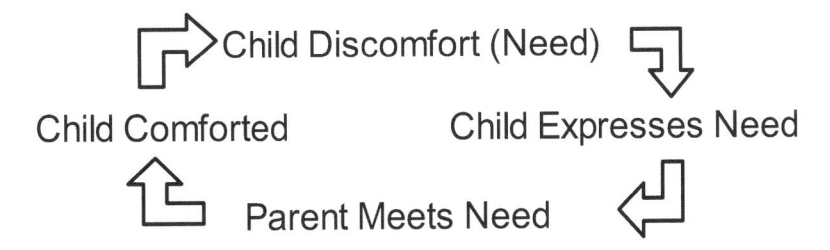

⇨ Child Discomfort (Need) ⇩

Child Comforted   Child Expresses Need

⇧ Parent Meets Need ⇦

Children form healthy and strong attachments by having their needs met on a continuous basis. Attachment is the channel through which a parent or caregiver is able to teach, pass on or help a child to grow throughout each development phase. Through this continual reliance, a child is able to build trust with their parent and is more willing to accept knowledge, insight and wisdom in support of their goals for each development phase.

Disruptions to an ongoing attachment process, such as from a parent being unavailable due to incarceration, may cause instability and trauma that will affect a child's ability to develop and form healthy attachments. When a child is separated from a parent, lives in an unstable environment or experiences poor parenting, they will not thrive emotionally or developmentally. Having continual discomfort (arising from not having their needs met), creates a situation where fear and insecurity develops. This fear, anxiety or stress will undermine the tasks and goals that need to be achieved in each stage of the development process.

The physical separation of one or more of the child's parents may also be sad and overwhelming to them. This will most likely impact them developmentally and influence their ongoing ability to form healthy long-lasting relationships. A secure attachment with each parent or caregiver creates a safe and nurturing environment where the child is able to fully develop emotionally, intellectually, socially and morally.

Children, almost always, have a strong desire to be connected to their families, even though their family situation may be far from perfect. They may have witnessed substance abuse, violence, neglect or any number of other distressing situations. Children with situations such as these, typically only want one thing - to remain at home with their families. While it may be conceptually difficult for us to understand, given their turbulent home environment, children have a very basic need and desire to remain attached to their parents.

This strong basic and unrelenting need of children speaks volumes about the strength of the attachment bond between children and their parents. When a child is separated from a parent, no matter what the circumstances, most children experience an extreme sense of loss. Even children who have never lived with one of their parents, for whatever reason, also experience the loss. These children often develop fantasies about how life would be with their missing parent and generally desire to live with them once they are released from prison. This once again indicates the strength and longevity of the desire to be attached to their parents.

It is often believed that incarceration of a parent breaks the attachment between a child and the parent. This is generally not true and statistics tell why. Over 75% of parents in state and federal prisons indicate that they have contact with their children after incarceration. Most of these parents indicated that they had frequent (monthly or more) contact with their children. Finally, about one-quarter of all incarcerated parents have frequent (monthly or more) visits with their children (even given the challenge that most facilities are far and difficult to get to).

So, why is parental or family attachment so important to a child? It provides them the means by which they meet their:
- Physical needs - food, housing, clothing, medical care
- Emotional needs - love, caring and acceptance
- Moral and Spiritual needs - rules for life, a belief system, religious practices
- Cultural needs - an understanding of family history, language, tradition and a sense of belonging

Parental and family attachment provides children with the sense of "who we are" or more specifically "who am I". It is through this basic parental or family attachment that children develop their basic beliefs, morals, spirituality, way of acting, family traditions and practices. Children develop a sense of belonging as they identify and embrace their parents, family and culture. Families, not only parents, play a large role in meeting a child's attachment needs.

Attachment plays another critical role in development of a child. It is the foundation for future relationships. When young children develop attachment issues or problems, they are more likely to have ongoing problems in relationships and with their behavior.

Attention should be focused on children who have experienced parental separations, basic parental losses or family disruptions because this type of "trauma" will interfere with their ability to attach. The following sections highlight the impact of attachment trauma for each of the child development phases.

A CHILD'S DEVELOPMENT NEEDS

For infants: the impact of attachment trauma may be less visible but is still very present. It is most often displayed through difficulty in sleeping and eating. Due to the fact that attachment and trust are basic or primary development tasks, trauma during the infancy, can play a large role in the ongoing development goals of children.

Attachment is an ongoing process and develops as a parent or caregiver meets and continues to meet a child's needs. Once a child is attached, the bonds become very strong over time. As a child grows the attachment grows, thus the importance for infants.

For infants, attachment develops from the parent or caregiver who provides for the basic physical needs of the child. Simple evidence of attachment development is demonstrated by the child's ability to tolerate short separations from their parents. If attachment is present, the child will trust that the parent will return. Over time, these periods of separation may grow longer because the child's trust also grows.

In order for this attachment to develop, perfect parenting does not have to be present. Even if a parent does not always meet their child's needs (due to emotional or physical separation from the child), the child will most likely continue to attach to the parent even though it may be at a slower pace than normal or desired.

Attachment is the primary task for infants who are between the ages of nine and eighteen months old. This is typically a period of "separation anxiety." A child may cry continually when a parent is not present. However, if the child has a healthy attachment to the parent, it is very likely that the child will be able to develop an alternative attachment to another caregiver who is consistently there to meet their needs.

It cannot be stressed enough that the most critical need for an infant is for a parent or caregiver that can consistently meet their needs. It is extremely helpful if the infant can continue to see the parent (who is incarcerated), especially if that child will eventually return to that parent's care. Under this situation and to the extent possible, an infant's daily routine should be maintained and changes kept to a minimum.

For early childhood children: the impact of parental separation can be very confusing. One of their primary development goals is to begin to separate from the parent and to start to learn more about the world. This task is made much more difficult when a parent is not present due to incarceration. The child is confused and may actually suffer developmental regression. How can a child separate from a parent, experimentally and safely, who is no longer there? How does a child gain the confidence to go out and discover new things in the world when they perceive it to be an unsafe place?

Early childhood children are developing additional language skills, basic independence and skills that will allow them to more take care of themselves. There are many foundational skills and behaviors that need to be learned during this development phase. The fact that these children often have difficulty understanding what happened with their incarcerated

A CHILD'S DEVELOPMENT NEEDS

parent creates confusion and fear and may keep them from fully attending to the development of their language skills. A lack in confidence and also the presence of low self-esteem may also contribute to delays in the development of these skills.

Children in this development phase often become very clingy, lack self-confidence and can be unsure of their decision making skills. Parents or caregivers need to tolerate this clingy nature as well as any potentially regressive behaviors. These children should be informed about where the parent is, be reassured that the parent is safe and also visit with the parent (as possible). They have a basic need to be continually assured that they will be cared for and loved and that they will be safe. Children in this development phase will be unable to move forward developmentally until they feel safe and secure. These children need lots of attention, reassurance and encouragement, all of which will help to build their confidence and self-esteem.

The parent of these children must be attentive to the child's perception of what has happened to their parent and to them. Most importantly, your child needs to fully understand and embrace the fact that what has happened to them is not their fault. Visits with the incarcerated parent will help them to more fully understand what has happened to them and their family. In order to overcome the potential for developmental delays, parents should be focused on their child's feelings of safety, security and trust (increasing their attachment foundation) as well as providing a predictable, consistent and understanding home environment.

For middle and late childhood children: the attachment trauma associated with parental separation interferes with their ongoing ability to learn, focus on tasks, and progress in school. In this age group, developmental goals typically include additional academic skills, peer friendships, more advanced physical capabilities and the development of their moral character.

Since these children may be preoccupied with what has happened to one of their parents, the development of their capabilities to understand and conceptualize may be impeded. In turn, their ability to perform in school may be hampered.

In addition, their development of peer friendships may suffer. This may be caused by the child's inability to articulate, what has happened to their parent, to their friends, or they may just be embarrassed by the event. They may also feel that their parent being gone is harsh or unfair and that they are confused to understand or explain why their parent is no longer home. Some children may even begin to make up stories about where their parent is, in order for them to rationalize their absence to themselves or save them from embarrassment with their friends.

Visits with their parent are important, for these children, not just for maintaining and growing a parental attachment, but also to help them understand more about prison and the legal system. Their ability to learn more about these things will help them in the development of their reasoning, as well as learn more about fairness and right versus wrong issues. If possible, the incarcerated parent should speak directly and honestly to the child about these issues.

Children in this age group begin to develop very strong feelings and will probably require help to deal with the confusion and anger that may be caused by the parental separation. Parents (not incarcerated) or caregivers need to be especially attentive to the child's relationships and problems that may arise from them feeling embarrassed or not knowing what to tell their friends.

For teenage children: developing their sense of identity and separating from parents and family are key development tasks. Typically, their ability to separate is based on the strength of their attachment to their parents - the stronger the attachment, the more willing they are to venture out and explore separation. If a parent is incarcerated, and a diminished attachment results, it can be a particularly confusing time for them as they have a weak attachment foundation supporting them.

The separation process is also exercised with their peer group. They seek to separate from their parents (and or family) and associate more strongly with their peer group. This process is also made more difficult when a child has a diminished attachment to one or more of their parents.

Teenagers, without a strong attachment foundation, typically struggle in adolescence as their desire for independence is impeded by a lack of a strong parental anchor. This may lead to confusion, anger, antisocial behavior and self-esteem issues.

Teenagers may also be impacted by parental incarceration due to the impact it plays on their peer relationships. These relationships are extremely important at this age, and may suffer due to the fact that the teenager may feel that they can't maintain their past friends (due to what their parent has done). Typically, in these situations, they seek out a new peer group – a group that traditionally has behavioral issues or that abuse drugs and alcohol, as a way to cope with their situation.

Teenagers, who are forced to move due to a parent's incarceration, struggle even more as they lose the attachment foundation they had with their former peer group. This compounds their attachment issues and intensifies any emotional instability, confusion or behavioral issues typically present in this development phase. Helping them to manage peer pressure is extremely important, as they may turn to drugs, alcohol or illegal behaviors to help them cope.

In order to assist teenagers struggling with these issues, the parent or caregiver should involve the teenager in as much planning, as possible, regarding their care and home environment. The more teenagers are able to have input into decisions, about their care, the better. Above all, teenagers need to feel empowered and that they have a voice and some sense of control in what is happening to them.

During a typical separation from their parent, teenagers are faced with many challenges. These challenges are best met if the teenager is able to still maintain contact with the incarcerated parent. They may have emotional issues with this parent, however having no contact removes any potential for a helpful attachment and will typically compound their emotional anxiety.

Depth:

A child's response to the separation trauma created from having a parent incarcerated varies according to their age and overall developmental progress. One of the major factors impacting a child's developmental progress is their emotional stability and ability to cope with changing family circumstances and events. Coping skills play a large role in a child's overall development progress. The depth and breadth of their attachments will play a key role in helping them with their ability to cope.

Coping with bad situations, such as an absent parent, is extremely difficult. A child's ability to cope is hampered by any levels of uncertainty surrounding their parental, family and home situation. Coping with a negative situation is hard enough but coping with uncertainty is even more difficult. Children in this situation are unsure if even the most basic of their attachment needs will be met, such as: "Who is going to care for me?" or "Is my dad okay?" or "Where am I going to live?".

Younger children are at the greatest risk because their coping skills are not yet fully developed. Older children, are more likely to act out behaviorally including rebellion, truancy or substance abuse.

Through "Depth" of attachment (with a non-incarcerated parent, a primary caregiver, strong family members, friends, role models, mentors, spiritual leaders and other caring influences), children can be introduced to a set of protective factors that will enable them to cope with parental incarceration more successfully.

These protective factors help a child to build resilience in the face of challenges, disappointments, peer pressure and uncertainty that typically arise from a parental incarceration. Depth will help them to face their challenges head-on, bounce back from setbacks, not to be overwhelmed as often, achieve difficult tasks and help them to overcome many of their specific emotional and life problems. Despite the difficulty of their circumstance, they may be able to heal, grow and learn from the adversity they have faced.

Protective factors that are consistently reinforced by a child's depth network, can enable a child to understand and embrace that it is not only about **what** happens to them in life, but it is more about **how they handle** the situation that really makes a difference. Protective factors include:

- **Positive Attachments** - healthy, positive relationships and involvement in constructive and supportive activities
- **Love and Care** - relationships that provide the child with the knowledge that someone is "there for me", "loves me" and also shows them they are part of a larger caring group, such as a family, a group of friends or church members
- **Defined Boundaries** - relationships that are based upon respect, agreed setting of values and expectations, self responsibility and consequences
- **Life Skills** - relationships that enable a child to learn about age-appropriate basic life skills, including: caring for themselves, money, relationships and working

- **High Expectations** - relationships that provide children with the sense that there are others who believe in them, who expect them to succeed and provide ongoing encouragement during difficult situations
- **Meaningful Membership** - opportunities for children to be heard, to be valued and become a meaningful member of a positively oriented group

Positive Attachments

Positive attachments are very important to children who have been separated from one or more of their parents. Positive attachments can include relatives, therapists, counselors, teachers, Big Brothers or Sisters, sports teams, after-school programs, clubs, part-time job (age-appropriate) or any other people or groups that provide healthy positive reinforcement for the child. Children also need help from these positive attachments, if appropriate, in order to maintain an active attachment with their incarcerated parent.

Love and Care

Love and care for children is critically important, especially if one of the child's parental attachments has been removed or severely diminished. In order to fill the gap, from this missing parental attachment, children need an abundance of unconditional love, care and support from healthy positive relationships.

Additional love and care relationships typically come from family members who have stepped in to fill the gap of the missing parent. They not only ensure that the basic physical needs of the child are taken care of but they can also focus on creating a nurturing environment for them. This includes providing empathy and encouragement - aimed at enabling the child to develop their unique identity - as well as enhance their positive self-worth and self-esteem.

Defined Boundaries

Specific and consistent boundaries are extremely important. Children need ownership of their behavior and need help in making decisions about appropriate behavior. The development of defined boundaries, and enforced consequences, will enable them to gain experience in making value decisions. Defined boundaries should include rules for home, school, relationships and home responsibilities. Defined boundaries will help children with safety, security, self-respect, independence and self-esteem.

Life Skills

The development of life skills are very important so that children may develop a sense of achievement, competence, work ethic and self-esteem as they progress through the goals of each development phase.

The development of life skills should include: goal setting and task development, physical care skills, home responsibilities, part-time work, career exploration, money management, and discussion of real life situations.

High Expectations

The development of high expectations are important for children with an incarcerated parent. Adults are often tempted to feel sorry for them, make things easier for them (since things are already so difficult) and not let them fully develop their current abilities. High expectations – combined with lots of encouragement - contribute to a child's development of work ethic, confidence, self-esteem and sense of achievement. Expectations should be set for home, school, sports, church, or any other goal related activity.

Positive attachments in the child's life should not only be nurturing but also be focused on helping the child to achieve successes (small and large). The child should be encouraged continuously (for each expectation of them) as their successes may be more difficult to achieve due to their situation. Do not let circumstances or challenges become an excuse for failure. Help create an environment where the child will experience success.

Meaningful Membership

Meaningful memberships are especially important to children so that they may learn and grow their life experiences, develop empathy for others and develop the realization that they can become a meaningful part of a larger group (family, team, church, etc.). Many children with an incarcerated parent have been exposed to illegal or harmful behaviors and meaningful membership in a positive group will help them to understand that healthy alternatives are not only available but to be sought out.

Meaningful membership can include mentoring relationships, teachers, sports activities, church membership, volunteer work, service projects or other activities where they will expand their life experience in a positive manner area.

The development of resilience, through depth of attachments, and the use of these protective factors, is not always directly related to the amount of trauma a child experiences. One would assume, the more trauma - the less resilience. This is not always true. This is a very encouraging point for children of incarcerated parents. Since a child can't control what has happened to them, it's extremely comforting for them to know that they can control how they deal with what has happened to them.

This is a very important responsibility for a parent or primary caregiver to remember. Since the children cannot be fully protected from life's traumas (parental separation, abuse, etc.), it is an attached adult's responsibility to help the child learn to live with the situation and to help them make a healthy recovery from the trauma. Developing a child's depth of attachments will spread the task of building a child's resilience onto a larger group. In this way, the burden is not totally on the remaining parent, family member or caregiver.

Long-term studies show that over half of children born into high-risk environments (poverty, war, abuse, violence, adoption) grow up to be not only successful (by worldly standards), but they also are typically described as confident, competent and caring. Research on the success rates of children of incarcerated parents is not specifically monitored, however the development of positive factors will definitely contribute to the development of resilience and that will play a key role in success rates of these children.

Depth of attachment and development of protective factors focus on a vulnerable child's developmental and behavioral risks. It also promotes the growth of healthy positive relationships to build resilience for overcoming the challenges associated with having an incarcerated parent.

Parents need to identify what is going right and what is working (strengths) with their child and focus their efforts on building more of what's going right into their child's life. Little may be able to be done to change their current situation or the risks arising from things that have occurred in the past. The availability of depth attachments exist in the present and those need to be built upon. You, nor your child, want to be defined by your current or past problems – a strong focus on protective factors will enable you to envision and implement a broader picture for your child's future.

Continually looking at the risks your child faces can sometimes become an overwhelming task and lead you or your child to give up. By developing a strong depth of attachment network, you and your child will have people that are focused on helping your child develop these key protective factors. They will definitely provide you and your child with a greater sense of strength, hope and resilience.

Conclusion

Through an in-depth understanding of your child's development goals, attachment relationships and depth of protective factors, parents and caregivers are more able to provide the things a child needs to help them overcome the trauma of a parental separation.

A child needs consistent and caring adults who can provide love, care and nurturing that is focused on their positive and healthy development. These adults need to be honest and open, with the child, and help them to express their feelings and learn to cope with them through positive - not negative outlets. Relationships with a child must carry goals, boundaries, encouragement and high expectations. A child, with an incarcerated parent, needs to be shown early and often that there are positive options available to them. They also need to understand that they can be a valuable contribution to something larger than themselves, such as to their family, church, club, sports team or school group.

- 2 -

Preparing to Parent from Prison

The majority of parents who are incarcerated are able to eventually reunite with their children. Even though you are presented with major challenges, it is very important to both you and your child, that you continue in your role as a parent. Both fathers and mothers play very critical roles in the development of their child's sense of security, identity and belonging - which will impact them throughout their entire lives.

A parent, who is incarcerated, typically has a number of major parenting related concerns, including: how to deal with the emotions of being separated from their child, making decisions regarding the care of their children, staying in contact with their child, and reuniting with their child once they are released from prison.

Parenting isn't easy. Parenting from prison is even harder, however, it is still very possible for you to play an active role in your child's life. Unfortunately, many incarcerated parents lose contact with their children and this does not have to happen. It will take a concerted effort on your part, and on the part of your child's other parent or caregiver, and maybe even the court.

Given the issues associated with remote parenting, you will probably be frustrated and feel overwhelmed at times. Communicating with your child, spouse and family has become more difficult given prison limitations. Due to the circumstances surrounding your incarceration, family relationships may even be strained. Despite these challenges, it is important that you continue to see yourself as a parent to your child. Parenting from prison is not easy, but it's not impossible either. It will require patience, creativity, and persistence on your part. Remember, being a parent is the most challenging and rewarding job you'll ever have.

Your child needs you to help them progress in their development, build strong healthy attachments and build resilience for their times of difficulty. Without your involvement your child is more likely, than other children, to have behavioral issues, academic problems, negative peers, and ongoing relationship problems. Often times, they experience higher levels of anxiety, fear and guilt which will impede their overall development process.

Being incarcerated does not mean that you have lost your right to make decisions about the care of your children or that your relationship with your child has become any less important. You can still be a good parent from prison: a parent that offers helpful advice, positive reinforcement and a sympathetic ear when your child needs someone to talk to.

You, and others, face everyday challenges in the raising of your child and each of these challenges can be overcome. In order to help you overcome these challenges, you need to spend time preparing: to understand yourself and your situation more fully, to know what impact your incarceration plays in your parenting role, to understand what struggles your child is facing, to fully appreciate what their development and attachment needs are, to know more about how your incarceration affects them, and to determine how you need to manage the relationship with their other parent or primary caregiver.

An incarcerated parent often feels that they must harness time so that time serves their needs while they're in prison. Some spend their time by joining groups, growing their spiritual walk, participating in sports or learning new skills. Some utilize the time to think more deeply about their lives. They reflect on the past: the things they've done and the things they have not done. They also think about the here and now: their current situation, their families and their ability to survive the prison environment.

Those with the emotional strength, think about the future. They think about how things can be, not how they are now. They look forward with hope, they plan for the future and envision the way things could be.

Hope requires emotional strength, perseverance and patience and is based on the real belief that there is a future for yourself, your child and your family. The ability to set, maintain and achieve goals is a direct result of having hope and believing that change is possible. Planning for the future means believing there is a future!

Many incarcerated parents turn to religion while in prison because of the fundamental principles of hope, faith and love that they are based upon.

This time of self reflection, hope and planning can allow an incarcerated parent an opportunity to develop honest, positive, constructive plans on how they can parent from prison. These plans may include how to stay in communication with your child, teaching your child morals and acceptable behaviors, developing cultural or racial pride within your child, explaining the difference between punishment and discipline, developing and maintaining healthy relationships as well as supporting the others who are providing primary support and care for your children.

Parenting from prison is not easy, however, it can be done. The number one thing that will help you - is for you to take responsibility for the consequences you have put upon your child. Initially, this may cause feelings of sadness and disappointment but these feelings can become the foundation for a commitment to understand and help the pain, fear and confusion your child is suffering. It is now up to you to "right the wrong" you have done to your child. After an initial period of grief (you can NOT get stuck here!), you can definitely move on. It can be a very energizing and empowering experience.

You may have some basic questions about how to prepare a plan to parent from prison. Let's review a few of the questions you might have.

How does being incarcerated change how I am a parent?

Physical separation obviously limits your ability to be a parent in the same way you did before. Even though you are still the child's parent, you won't be handling day-to-day decisions, participating in routine activities, or providing discipline to your child. While this may leave you with a sense of loss, confusion and even helplessness, you still can provide them with emotional support, life guidance and encouragement – these things are very important to them!

You can also be actively involved in helping make important decisions about their lives. It is important to understand that you can still be an active and caring parent even though you are not in the home. Your child is dealing with a lot in their life and they will need as much time and support from you as possible.

Is it too late to establish a relationship with my child?

Even if you weren't that involved or never had much contact with your children, prior to your incarceration, it's never too late to develop a relationship with them. Often while in prison, a parent's priorities change greatly and they seek to correct past relationship mistakes. Beginning or rebuilding of a relationship, with your child, from prison may be complicated and slow but it is not impossible. It will take many small steps, to build trust and attachment, rather than one large leap.

Before you take any steps to reestablish your relationship, it is extremely important that you think through the long term commitment that you must make in order to be a consistent parent to them. It is very hard and unfair to have a parent who drops in and out of their lives. Once you've made this commitment, you'll need to contact the child's primary caregiver to determine how open they are to this and if the emotional state of the child is prepared for this step. Given past relationships, with the caregiver and your child, this step may require patience and perseverance on your part and any open issues would need to be resolved before moving forward. It is very important to remember that establishing or rebuilding a relationship takes time and trust. Move forward slowly, gently and respectfully.

What affects how my children react to my incarceration?

The way your children might react to your being in prison is complicated. Each child is different and will react differently. In addition, their feelings and behaviors also change over time. Some of the things that may play an influencing role on them are:

- their age and the length of your prison stay
- their relationship with you prior to your incarceration
- their relationship with their current caregiver
- the stability of their home life
- if they were living with you prior to your incarceration
- their knowledge and feelings about your crime
- if they are separated from their brothers and sisters
- how they are now treated because you are in prison
- the amount and quality of contact they have with you

The way a child reacts is often based on the changes that occur in your relationship with them during your prison stay. These changes occur during three major phases: 1) the initial separation from you at the time of your incarceration, 2) the ongoing separation between you and them, and 3) the reunification period after your release.

How can I cope emotionally from being separated from my child?

How you deal with your incarceration will have a direct influence on how your child will cope with it. You may be experiencing regret, depression, loss, guilt, embarrassment, anxiety or even helplessness because of the separation. You may be afraid of being rejected by your children, that they will be resentful to you or that they may attach to someone else during your absence. Your child needs you to help them during this adjustment period, so you need to first deal with your emotions - so you will then be able to support their emotional needs.

All of your emotions can have a negative impact on your child. It is extremely important that you try and deal with these emotions so that you can be a healthy, positive influence during the limited contact you have with them. This is not to say that you should be dishonest or hide your feelings, however you need to consider the most constructive way to present your feelings, should the situation arise. For example, it is okay that you tell them that you are disappointed with your behavior (that got you into prison) but that it has been an opportunity for you to learn and grow from it - not that it has become a disabling emotion to you.

How are my children impacted by me being in prison?

This can be a difficult question given the factors mentioned above. Each child and situation is different, however research shows that children separated from a parent due to incarceration display some common behavioral and emotional reactions. Behavioral reactions can include:
- sleeping problems or nightmares
- problems in school (focus grades, fights, etc.)
- withdrawal from family and friends
- lying or making up stories
- drug or alcohol abuse
- breaking the law
- regressive activities (behavior of younger children)
- rebellion arising from changes to or new living situations

Emotional reactions can include:
- grief, sadness, loneliness or depression (from separation)
- low self-esteem and low confidence levels (feel rejected)
- rejection & guilt or shame & embarrassment
- confusion or helplessness
- fear, worry or anxiety (about your and their safety)
- anger (towards you, "the system", or their caregiver)
- lack of trust or fear of attachment
- expectation of rejection in relationships

How can I prepare to work on my relationship with my child?

Find out as much as you can about your child's day-to-day life. Stay in close contact with your spouse, primary caregiver or family members (especially in your attachment network) and find out how your child is really doing, what is their emotional state, how their behavior is, how they're doing in school, who their friends are and what activities are they involved in. This will also help you feel more connected to what is really going on in their lives.

Acknowledge your feelings. It's okay to express your feelings, however you need to consider the best way to present your feelings (age-appropriate ones) to your children. If you ignore or deny your feelings, you may not be able to react in the most healthy and positive way which your child needs. It's important that you be careful about sharing all of your emotions with your children. Although it's very important to be honest with your children and to explain how you're feeling to them, remember that your child may take your feelings personally. It may help to maintain a journal, so that you can reflect more thoughtfully on your feelings and be able to see how you've changed, over time, in the expression or management of your feelings.

Take inventory. You should take an inventory of your personal strengths and positive attributes. This will serve as a reminder to you of the assets you bring to the relationship with your child and the ways you can help them as they develop.

Talk to other incarcerated parents. They may have overcome some similar challenges and can help you with yours.

They may also bring a different perspective that can help you see things in a slightly different light.

Work on your support system. Your child needs depth of attachments (family, friends, spiritual leaders, teachers, mentors, chaplain, counselor's, etc.), so you need to be in communication with them, in order to build and maintain this network. For the sake of your child, even if your relationship with their other parent is over, you need to establish and maintain a positive relationship with them. Be prepared to make amends and apologize where necessary.

Learn more about parenting. Utilize the library, parenting programs and any other materials that you can get a hold of to help you learn more about child development, parenting and relationships.

Set realistic goals. Develop a plan with realistic goals about what you are going to do, how you're going to do it, what involvement will look like with your child, and what other resources (family, friends, etc.) that you'll need to utilize.

Learn to be patient. This is a stressful time for all concerned - you, your child, your spouse or caregiver, your family, etc. Some things will take time to achieve (trust and attachment are achieved slowly) and will require steady, consistent action on your part. Children need to know that you won't give up and that you will be there for the long term.

Reduce your stress. Take up activities that reduce stress: exercise, prayer, meditation, music, etc. You need to have the right frame of mind and a positive mental outlook so you can do your best in rebuilding and maintaining a relationship with your child.

How can I use my Bible for guidance?

The Bible is rich in guidance for how to raise your children. It is also highly encouraged for you as well, so that you can develop an appropriate emotional and spiritual state. Besides the general wisdom of "loving the Lord your God" and "loving one another" there are a number of Books in the Bible that provide wisdom for raising children. The following areas provide a strong foundation which can guide you and your relationship activities with your child. Bible use should always be supplemented with lots of prayer.

- Be a Godly example - Proverbs 1:7-9, Proverbs 20:7
- Show unconditional love - Proverbs 4:1-4, Luke 15:20
- Encourage them - Proverbs 3:21-26
- Provide wise instruction - Proverbs 2:1-7 & 22:6
- Provide reasonable boundaries - Proverbs 6: 20-23
- Provide a sympathetic ear - Proverbs 18:13-15
- Create a happy environment – Proverbs 15:13-17

Building Your Plan

As parents, there are two main areas where you can have the greatest influence on your child's life:

affirmation and encouragement - for them to have hope and self-esteem. For each development goal, personal activity, homework, test, success or achievement - to let them know what a great job they did and how important they are to you, their family, their friends, their church, their team, etc.

guidance and support – provide wisdom and help in order to guide them through each development phase of their life and eventually to help them develop plans, goals, and life skills that they will need throughout their adult life.

In order to provide appropriate affirmation and encouragement, you'll need to have a good understanding of what type of things they're doing: at home, at school, in church, sports, with family, etc. This means that you will need to have regular, thoughtful, affirming and consistent contact with them, they're other parent or caregiver, and any other meaningful attachments. Consistent contact will include phone conversations, personal visits (if available), cards and letters to them.

If you are going to provide guidance and support, you'll need to understand as much as you can about where they are in each development phase, what their goals, traits and behaviors are for that development phase, as well as what activities, interests and any academic activities that they may be involved in. If you encounter issues in being able to get all the information you need, talk or write to other members of your child's attachment network to get the information you need. Stay connected on as many fronts as possible.

One of the foundational steps of being an encouragement to your child is to tell your child that you love them, frequently. Children, dealing with separation trauma, can be very fragile and may not know how you really feel. In each contact you have with them, it is very important to tell them how much you love them.

Don't be surprised if they don't respond in the same way, they may be confused, angry or dealing with other emotions and they are not ready to respond accordingly.

From what you have now read about development, attachment, depth, and what issues you may be facing, it's now time put together your Parenting Plan. You'll be determining what your child needs and what you can specifically do to support those needs in a positive, encouraging and healthy way.

On the following pages, a sample Parenting Plan has been provided to assist you in the process of getting started. After the example, there is a blank worksheet that you can use to build a plan specifically for your child. Take your time on the plan; refer back to materials throughout the entire book frequently.

You'll need to modify your child's plan over time (probably every six months or so) as your child ages, advances developmentally (use chapter 1 development table), changes their ongoing activities and if there have been any behavioral changes.

Be specific as possible - list what you are going to do - commitment is the key – your child needs to know that you care, that you will be consistent and that you will follow through with things you have promised.

Parenting Plan

Date:_____   Page: 1

	My child's needs/goals:
Developmental Phase: Middle Childhood - Age: 7	Some independence, basic reasoning skills, ownership of actions/behaviors/promotions, start of work ethic and self productiveness.

Things I need to do: in conjunction with his primary caregiver, I will help to set-up a chore and behavior list. I will encourage him in letters, visits and calls about how special he is and I will praise him about specific, positive accomplishments that he has made.

Emotional: Basic & Possible Issues	Some control over self and emotions, minor rebellion in order to test independence, anger over my situation, need for some control over minor decisions.

Things I need to do: during calls and visits, I will talk about what problems he is having and I will listen to his input. I will let him know that his input and feelings will be taken into consideration and that he is an important member of our family.

Attachment	Understanding that his physical needs will be met during this time of family struggle. Understanding that, if I could, I would be at home to be with him. That he understand that he is an important member of our family.

Things I need to do: I will be reassuring during each letter, visit and phone call that we (as a family) are going to be there for him no matter what and that by working together, our family, will come through this situation just fine. I will reassure him that I am doing okay and that I am safe. I will tell him in each communication with him that I miss him, love him and wish I could be home with him.

Parenting Plan

Date: _____   Page: 2

	My child's needs/goals:
Depth:	The need for positive relationships to fill the gap while I am gone. Relationships that encourage and build its positive expectations for him. The need for chores (that teach life skills), rules and consequences. The need for a "go-to" person (other than my spouse) in my absence. The need for someone to be my "eyes and ears".

Things I need to do: I will write letters to my mother, brother and mother-in-law and ask them about my child's progress and if they will send me a short note about how they think things are going. I will write a letter to my child, and send it to my mother, and ask her to read it to my son.

Interests:	Soccer, friends, reading, music

Things I need to do: I will write each week about his soccer team and ask him to write me back, letting me know how he and the team are doing. During each phone call or visit, I will ask and encourage him about his reading and music activities. I will ask about his friends and have him tell me about them. Once a quarter, I will write a story for him.

Spiritual:	Needs to belong to a church and in a Bible study class and develop friends from church.

Things I need to do: I will find one or more of my family members who will take my son to church and Bible study regularly. I will write them once a month to thank them and see how I can help them. I will read what my son is studying in Bible study and discuss it with him during phone calls, visits, and letters.

Parenting Plan

Date: _____   Page: 3

	My child's needs/goals:
Dates to Remember:	Birthday, start of school, school events, Christmas, Valentine's Day.

Things I need to do: I will make or buy cards for each of these events and mail them at least one week prior to the event. I will tell him special he is and how much I miss him in each card.

Misc:	Schoolwork, after-school projects, family events.

Things I need to do: I will encourage him to keep up with his homework in each letter or phone call. I will discuss homework challenges and encourage him during personal visits. I will ask his primary caregiver for homework updates during our weekly calls. I will assist in teaching him should there be any areas his caregivers might be struggling with.

Other:	

Things I need to do:

Parenting Plan

Date:_____   Page: 1

My child's needs/goals:	
Developmental Phase:	
Things I need to do:	
Emotional:	
Things I need to do:	
Attachment	
Things I need to do:	

Parenting Plan

Date: _____   Page: 2

	My child's needs/goals:
Depth:	
Things I need to do:	
Interests:	
Things I need to do:	
Spiritual:	
Things I need to do:	

Parenting Plan

Date: _____   Page: 3

	My child's needs/goals:
Dates to Remember:	
Things I need to do:	
Misc:	
Things I need to do:	
Other:	
Things I need to do:	

- 3 -

What a Child Asks

A developing child will ask lots of questions. Your developing child, with you being incarcerated, will ask even more questions. Their questions and your answers will become a key part of the ongoing relationship that you have with your child. This relationship will require and thrive on honesty and genuineness from you.

A child needs genuine caring parents who provide love, encouragement and nurturing. They need honesty, even when they have been exposed to or are undergoing bad situations, so that they can learn to understand their situation, express their feelings and develop coping skills.

There is often a negative stigma associated with a parent's incarceration, and in many cases, may cause parents, caregivers and family to make a concerted effort to conceal the truth from the child, their friends and others in the community - thinking they are helping to protect the child. This "concealing of the truth" can take several forms: it's something the family "doesn't talk about", the child is provided with very little information, the child is given no reason or false reasons why their parent is gone, or they are deceived entirely and told a false story.

Parents, caregivers or family often try to justify this dishonesty by saying the child is "too young to understand", they fear the child will "follow in their parent's footsteps", or that they are "just trying to protect them" from the negative stigma that will come from their friends, teachers, etc.

Parents and family need to understand, however, that a child with false or limited knowledge of their parent's situation will typically react negatively. Some react with fear – a fear that arises from the fact that their friends or others know more about what has happened and that they may hold this against them. Other children struggle with coping – by not having the knowledge or understanding of the reality of their parent's absence, they don't know what to feel - creating a state of emotional confusion.

If a child is not given an answer or plausible explanation, they will often fantasize about what has happened or create their own explanation to fill the void left by not knowing the truth. This may have unintended consequences. The child may blame themselves. They may feel they have done something wrong that sent their parent away. They may withdraw from family or peer relationships in order to avoid the embarrassment of not knowing what to say or out of a fear that their explanation may be shown to be wrong.

Incomplete or false information may lead a child to blame themselves and feel that they have done something wrong, something that has contributed to their parent being away. This forces the child to internalize the situation - thereby creating an emotional stigma and guilt. These feelings typically impede normal emotional development.

One of the important emotional developmental aspects of being honest with your children is that it will enable them to separate "your actions" from "their actions". This separation provides an opportunity for them to avoid potential feelings of blame, guilt or shame - thereby helping them to progress along a more normal emotional development path.

You have to remember that children are very smart. While they may be able to be convinced that the parent is away for some other reason (rather than the real one), there are a number of risks in taking this approach. They may become confused by discrepancies between what they are told and what they see or experience. The child may lose trust - with those people who are very important attachments - when – NOT IF - the truth does come out. It is generally much better for a child to find out from their parent, or caregiver or other family member, what the truth really is, rather than find out in a potentially negative environment - from friends or other people who care much less about their emotional well-being.

In telling the child, about a parent's incarceration, it is important to keep the explanation simple and age-appropriate. The explanation should include a number of very important points:

- that the incarcerated parent loves and cares for the child
- that the incarceration is in no way the fault of the child
- that the incarceration is due to the incarcerated parent making a mistake
- about how long the incarcerated parent will be away
- how contact will be maintained with the incarcerated parent (phone, mail, visits)

Obviously, there may be a number of overriding factors that determine the answers to the above points, including: court or sentencing provisions, stage of the incarceration process, parental and family relationships, the prison facility and its location, etc. Some of the items will require time and preparation in order to address them accurately and honestly - some may just take time to find out. It would be better to say that you don't know and that you will find out rather than provide inaccurate information.

Some children will ask additional questions when you tell them about your incarceration. Others may wait and ask questions, later, as they begin to process the information and their feelings. They may also need guidance in dealing with any stigma or teasing that may arise from their peers. They will need help with coming to terms with what has happened - to them, to you and to their family. Children need a safe place to express their fears and feelings, and find answers to their questions.

You also need to be attentive to any attitudes and behaviors that you may unknowingly be passing along to your child during your explanation. They should clearly understand that a prison is not a normal place to be and that criminal behavior is not appropriate. The objective of explaining and talking with your child is so that you can enable them to normalize their experience and feelings without normalizing crime or prison. You may want to consider the use of an emotional care specialist to assist you in sorting through your feelings and attitudes and with the development of an emotionally appropriate explanation.

Children may also need guidance in dealing with the prison stigma and any teasing that they may get from their peers. If they are told not to share the information of their parent's incarceration, they need a plausible explanation to share with others. Nowadays, children are quite aware and accepting of single-parent families and children living with other family members or caregivers. It might be enough to tell your child that they can tell others that their "parents are separated". Research has shown a striking similarity in the responses and concerns between children of incarcerated parents and those with separating/divorcing parents.

Prior to looking at specific questions your child may ask you, there are a number of things you should review in order to prepare yourself for answering questions with your child.

Open lines of communication - your child is going to have many questions - over many days and months. It is extremely important that you keep open all lines of communication with them – through letters, phone calls and visits. You'll need all of these channels in order to communicate effectively with them.

Age-appropriate answers - your answers to their questions will depend mostly on how old they are. As your child gets older, they may ask more complex questions and want more detailed information. Be prepared to discuss and answer questions about your incarceration and any concerns your children may have. It is very important to remember that their fears are real and uncertainty causes stress in children. Prepare to provide them with answers that they can understand. After you tell them, you might want to have them repeat the answer back to you – in their own words, to make sure they really understood.

Children and their feelings - children of all ages sometimes have problems in talking about their feelings. They may be confused about them, unsure about them or not know how to express how they feel. Remember, they are trying to cope with a lot, too. Their emotions are very real to them - even if they don't make sense to you. Listen closely to what your children are saying. If you're not sure, ask them questions about how they feel.

There are generally four primary questions that children most often ask or want to ask an incarcerated parent:

- **Where are you?**
- **Why are you there?**
- **Are you okay?**
- **When are you coming home?**

These questions can come in many forms. Many children, especially those in late childhood or older, ask them directly in a straightforward way. Other children, especially younger ones, avoid direct questions out of fear, embarrassment or confusion. Some children even act out their questions through aggressive behavior, getting into trouble or direct confrontation with a parent or caregiver.

A child's incarcerated parent, the other parent or caregiver and any other attached (or to be attached) adult should be fully prepared to answer these questions. Many times parents or other adults are uncomfortable with having this conversation. This discomfort has to be overcome and preparation is needed in order to answer the questions in ways that the child will understand.

While non-incarcerated parents and other attached adults should be prepared to answer these questions, it is your responsibility – as the incarcerated parent – to be the one to answer most of these questions. Your child will typically gather more information than just the simple answer to the question. They'll see or hear the feelings of the incarcerated parent, they'll ask follow-up questions about your experience and it is also an opportunity for you to tell your child how much you love them and miss them.

Sometimes however, the responsibility for answering these questions will fall on the other parent or caregiver. In these instances, children seem to respond best when the questions are answered in a simple, straightforward and honest way.

As difficult and painful as this time may be, it is a critically important time to your child. When they better understand the situation they, their parent and their family are going through, the quicker they will be able to adjust and resume a more normal emotional development process.

Each of the questions a child asks is of critical importance to them. The following section will more closely examine each question and review a range of responses that you may want to consider when developing a plan to discuss them with your child.

Where are you?

Parents or caregivers often try to protect child by avoiding the truth about where the incarcerated parent really is. There are a number of common stories often used by parents, caregivers and family members to answer the child's question of "where are you?" Let's first review these and why they typically don't work.

Working far away - this may satisfy your child's question at first, however, they may see the family strain financially (due to a parent's incarceration) and be confused or not understand why money is tighter when the parent is away at work. They don't understand why a parent would not send money home or come home to visit on weekends, holidays or vacations.

Away at school - this story rarely succeeds, especially with school age children, who are old enough to understand that people (even college students) come home from school occasionally. Children of incarcerated parents often have trouble in school and could develop a negative association with school because they may link parental separation and school in a negative way.

Joined the military - while this may appear to provide the child with a very plausible explanation for their parent's absence (especially to their friends), it can be difficult to explain particularly if a parent's sentence is short. In addition, it may cause excessive fear and worry as they believe their parent may be in danger or involved in a war situation.

In the hospital - this story may again bring fear, worry and anxiety about their absent parent. Given the possible long period of time that a parent may be away, a child's imagination may start to take over and they can worry about why they have not returned - even to the point where they imagine that their parent has died and no one is telling them the truth.

Regardless of the story, sooner or later any dishonesty will eventually be exposed to the child. They are most likely to overhear a conversation that will reveal the truth. They may see mail from the absent parent which will have been clearly marked as coming from a correctional facility. The truth tends to trickle down to friends, neighbors or teachers, etc. and eventually someone will reveal the truth to your child - many times in a negative or unhealthy way.

Once the child realizes the truth, they feel lied to. They begin to develop a distrust that will hurt not only your relationship but also their relationships in general. Strong attachments are built on strong foundations of trust. Lying is generally intended to minimize a child's feelings of shame or embarrassment (associated with the parent's imprisonment), however, once the lie is discovered the child's attachment and trust abilities are weakened.

In addition to creating a potentially large trust issue with the person or group who told the lies, these stories will inhibit your ability to maintain the necessary communication with your child and this is critical for the development of a healthy parent/child relationship. Using stories such as those above, letters and personal visits to the prison would be out of the question. Ongoing contact is fundamental to a parent/child relationship.

Upon arriving at the decision to tell your child the truth, you'll want to be prepare to answer your child's questions in a way which will be age appropriate. Younger children (early childhood and younger) don't generally understand what a prison is or why someone would be sent to prison. With them, give them basic details - details you're fairly certain that they'll understand. You can always provide more information as they get older. As a general rule, you can tell that your child is ready for more detailed information when they start to ask you more complicated questions.

For middle childhood children (7-10), they may begin to seek more information and ask more questions. Around 7 or 8 years old, children begin to develop a sense of right and wrong. They may begin to understand what a prison is and that people are sent to prison because they did something wrong. Typical responses could include, "I did something wrong and can't come home for a while" or "I made a mistake and now have to pay for that mistake".

Once a child has been told about where their absent parent is, the next related question is what do they tell others? Parents and caregivers generally have three choices: tell the truth and let it be out in the open, have your child keep it quiet, or make up a story. Parents and caregivers (it is often encouraged to involve a professional counselor) have to judge the potential benefits and dangers of each option to a child's emotional health.

While telling the truth is generally the preferred option, your child may be asked inappropriate questions or teased by other children. Prior to making this decision, it is important that you review your child's emotional strength and attachment support network to determine if they are strong enough emotionally (and also have supportive resources readily available to them) to handle any potential negative situation. In addition, your child should be prepared – by you, your spouse or the child's counselor - in advance to handle the questions they will be faced with when they tell the truth to others.

Some parents encourage their child not to disclose the entire truth, to others, about where their absent parent really is. This may not necessarily be poor advice, since other children can be very cruel - they may tease, reject or humiliate your child. Once again, the advice of a professional counselor could be sought out. Consideration should be given to the fact that when a child has no one (especially peers) to share their feelings and concerns with, it can take an emotional toll on them.

By talking with and asking some questions and finding out what's going on in your child's life, you can help prepare them so that they feel somewhat more comfortable about what they say to other people or their friends. Talking with them, ahead of time, can help them to prepare for many of the potentially awkward or uncomfortable situations that they may find themselves in or be faced with.

Understandably, it is a difficult decision and process to be honest with your child and tell them that you are incarcerated. The potential to allow parental shame or fears - that your child may think less of you - should not be allowed to enter into the decision-making process. Your feelings, while important, should not take precedence over the long term emotional development of your child.

Once your child knows the truth of **where** you are, the next question they usually ask is **why**.

Why are you there?

The next step in helping your child to avoid the potential for emotional confusion and also to help them make sense out of what has happened, they need to know why you are in prison. If they don't, they may become overly nervous and anxious as they may feel it had something to do with them.

Most children understand the concept of being punished or having consequences for breaking rules. Young children, however, need more simple descriptions for what happened such as, "I stole something", "I took drugs" or "I sold drugs". Older children will have more detailed questions and will require more detailed answers.

Truth can be much easier on a child than you imagine. Most children hear things about crime on TV, on the street, within the home or within the family. Knowing you're in prison but lacking the knowledge about why, may confuse your child (especially concerning trust, honesty, basic concepts of right and wrong, fairness, justness, etc.) and possibly hinder their ability to express their true feelings. They may also feel that they are only being told "part of the truth" and thereby creating basic trust issues with you.

The fundamental point that children should be told is that people are sent to jail or prison because they did not obey the law. They should be told that laws are rules that tell us how people should and should not behave. This should be a concept that your children are familiar with, as they probably will already have rules of behavior. For younger children, they may be aware that when they break the rule, they may get a timeout or lose privileges. They should be able to easily understand that prison or jail is like a long time out for adults.

For older children, it is important that you emphasize the role you played that lead to your incarceration. Children generally understand the fact that everyone makes mistakes and that mistakes often carry consequences. Your ability to take ownership of the choices you made will play an important role in your child's ability to develop their value system, concepts of right and wrong and that rules and consequences will play an important part of their life.

On occasion, some incarcerated parents are innocent or sentenced harshly. For them and their family, there may be an underlying feeling of anger, frustration and unfairness. This may also create a feeling of hopelessness and despair within the family and be passed along to the children. This type of situation should be talked about with your child, however you need to be conscious of several factors. First, not to undermine a child's respect for rules, appropriate behavior and the legal system. Second, not to create, in them, a sense of lingering fear or distrust of the system. Finally, to help your child learn positive ways to overcome unfairness, unjustness or those events which led up to the current situation. Extreme care should be exercised in these situations as children with an incarcerated parent generally are overly concerned about and attached to the remaining parent or caregiver. They may develop a fear that they too will be taken away. Too much talk about how unfair or unjust the system is, will only create additional fear with the child.

Many incarcerated parents, who are guilty of their crime, struggle with the fear of being rejected by their loved ones if they know the truth. So, they lie in order to try to keep their families intact. The truth will eventually come out at some point in the future and create honesty and trust issues with those who have been lied to.

Upon learning the truth, some children are extremely angry. They are upset that their parent would break the law, and risk going to prison, rather than not break the law and be able to be at home with them. They may also have a feeling of abandonment. In most cases, you need to sincerely and honestly apologize to your child for the upset and disruption that you have caused. You also need to sincerely seek your child's forgiveness and ask them to be a partner in helping to rebuild your relationship.

It takes courage, hope, prayer and strength to have this conversation with your child. It means risking anger, conflict and rejection. It means admitting that you have caused pain to those you love. Your commitment to overcoming these fears and to have perseverance in facing these issues will directly impact your ability to rebuild and sustain a relationship with your child during and after your incarceration.

Once your child knows the truth of **where** you're at and **why** you're there, the next question they usually ask is **when** will you be back.

When are you coming home?

During the legal process, from initial arrest to release from prison, there is typically a great amount of uncertainty about when you will come home. Most often, you know that there are a range of possible outcomes that can happen, such as: bail or no bail, plea bargains, sentencing guidelines, early release, etc. and specific times and dates are difficult to know with certainty.

Arising from denial or hope, you may have the desire to reassure your child that you will be out soon. It is a parent's natural response to want to provide comfort to a distressed child who is begging you to come home. The natural response is "soon" or "it won't be very long now".

Not only are "soon" and "it won't be very long now" open to a wide set of expectations but a child's concept of time is generally very different than an adult's. A child, who is expecting a parent to come home from prison, at a certain time, can be devastated when the parent fails to arrive. Once again the foundation of attachments and trust, can be severely diminished when this occurs.

Your child will most likely be able to handle the uncertainty of a your release date when they have honest answers - even if that means telling them "I really don't know."

Once a level of certainty is known regarding a release date, specific information should be given to the child. Younger children are generally unable to grasp the concept of things being "years" away. With them, it's easier to relate a parent's return in terms of seasons, birthdays or holidays. For example, "I will be home after you have four more birthdays."

Remember, longer sentences sound long no matter how you try to soften it. "I will come home when you are 18" is truly a lifetime to a 6 year old. Children can think in concrete terms, though – so the truth is generally much easier for them to grasp than a vague answer like "I will be gone a long time."

Consideration, when discussing **when** are you coming home issues, should be given to where home is really going to be. In many situations, parents being released will not be living with their child. Children of incarcerated parents often fantasize or imagine wonderful or "longed for" reunions with their parents or families. Parents and caregivers should be honest with the child regarding what the family unit will be or is intended to be upon the your release.

Once your child knows the truth of **where** you are, **why** you are there and **when** you will be out, the next question they usually ask is **are you okay**.

Are you okay?

For the most part, your child just wants to be reassured that you are safe and are able to manage during this difficult time. Most children know, even the younger ones, that prison is an unpleasant and undesirable place to be.

Most incarcerated parents would like to assure their child that they are safe and happy, but unfortunately, they cannot. Prison is not an "okay" place to be. Answering the question of "are you okay" should relate the fact that prison is "not okay" but that you are able to handle it. Answers could be phrased like:

"I'm not okay being in here but I can certainly handle it"

"I'm okay in some ways - I have a bed and food - but I am not okay because prison is not a good place to be"

"I'm okay – but it's not okay because I can't be with you"

Your answer should balance the truth about prison not being an okay place with some reassurance that you are not in danger and that you miss them very much. They need to know that you are still going to be a part of their life, even if you are not presently in the home with them.

Children are very sensitive to their own environment and those that have been able to visit with an incarcerated parent, gain a deeper sense of what a really difficult environment prison can be. Without reassurance from you, your child may develop an unnecessary emotional burden - worry and anxiety.

It is also not necessary to tell children about all of the negative and difficult aspects of being in prison in order to help them learn that prison is a major punishment and a very undesirable place to be. Sharing these negative things will only tend to worry them more.

There are also two other questions that are in your child's heart and mind, but that they rarely ever ask you:

- **Do you love me?**
- **Do you blame me for what happened?**

These are questions that children typically do not ask directly but that they are always seeking to have answered.

Two of your primary goals, in the emotional development of your child during your incarceration, are to insure that your child does in fact feel loved by you (and by others that are in your child's depth network) and that they don't feel responsible - in any way - for the circumstances in which they and their family now find themselves.

A child will often interpret an incarcerated parent's behavior solely in connection to themselves. Often times, you may not see the connection between your criminal activity and how it impacts your child's emotional makeup. For example, your child may think "If you loved me you wouldn't have gone to jail (abandoned me)." Obviously, you certainly didn't commit a crime for the purpose of abandoning your child or family, however from your child's eyes they may see it that way. You should be unwavering in your assurance that you love your child deeply and unconditionally. You should tell them that you love them often.

A child may face a lot of changes in their life when a parent goes to jail or prison. This could create a feeling of insecurity.

You may be able to provide them with some answers regarding the potential changes in their life, but in situations where you can't answer their questions, you'll need to reassure them that they are loved (not only by you but also by all the other attachments they have) and that they will be cared for no matter what.

A child may often blame themselves for their incarcerated parent's situation. The reasons may vary widely and be complex emotionally. Examples include: the child who pressured their parents for an expensive gift can think that the parents subsequent arrest was related to an effort to get the desired object, a child may have been angry at their parent and believe that the subsequent arrest was somehow related to their negative thoughts. Your child needs continual reassurance that they did nothing to cause your incarceration.

It is very important for you to provide your child with a safe and nurturing environment to express their feelings, thoughts, and beliefs about why you have been incarcerated. This may take several forms, including time talking with you, with their other parent, with other important attachments or even with a professional counselor or therapist. It is important that your child realize that there are negative consequences when a parent breaks the law and that they are not responsible for their parent's behavior or the subsequent consequences.

- 4 -

Visiting with Your Child

One of the very important elements of building and maintaining a child/parent relationship, while you are incarcerated, is direct contact with you child through visitation – if allowable and in the best interest of your child. Personal visits, however infrequent or restricted, are still one of the most effective ways to communicate, relate and attach to your child.

Some people believe that it may be too traumatic for a child to visit with a parent who is in prison. Many children, however, can benefit from contact with their parent; even if it occurs in a prison. Every child is different, but generally the sooner a child can have contact with their incarcerated parent, the better. Although a visit can be emotionally trying for your child, the long-term benefits may outweigh any potential short-term difficulties.

Personal visits, allow you to more closely relate with your child – to express your love for them and to see how they are growing and developing. You are also able to see their body language and expressions, have personal contact (if permissible) through hugs, etc. They can also see personally how you're doing, and together you'll create relationship experiences that both of you can draw upon in the future.

Your ability to closely relate with your child will play a fundamental role in your ability to build, grow and maintain a strong relationship with them. Personal visits play a key role your relationship building and in the overall development of your child. Some of the key objectives and benefits of personal visits, include:

Letting your child know their loved - love and care for your child are fundamental components to a healthy parental relationship with your child. Your primary goal is to help your child to feel worthy and lovable. You can accomplish this through lots of unconditional love, empathy, understanding, encouragement and affirmation. Unconditional love involves loving your child for who they are (and telling them that often) - not necessarily for what they do (praising positive behaviors is good but is not quite the same as unconditional love). Empathy and understanding involves listening to their problems, feelings and concerns and being able to relate with them on an emotional level so that they know that you know what they are going through. Encouragement and affirmation involves praising them for their unique identity and self-worth as well as promoting self-esteem, high expectations and a positive work ethic. While physically caring for your child may be limited, due to your incarceration, you can assume certain responsibilities for ensuring that their physical needs are met by others and that you are aware of and take responsibility for any problems which they may have.

Establishing prison reality with your child - when your child doesn't know your actual condition or circumstances, they often begin to imagine how things might be. In many cases, their imagination is more likely to be much worse and more frightening than reality. As scary and dismal as the prison and the prison visiting room may be, it is most likely far better than what your child imagines. While you may be disheartened at having to share this environment with them, they should adapt over a reasonably short period of time. The ability to remove uncertainty, worry and anxiety, about how you are doing, will potentially reduce or remove a number of emotional and developmental stumbling blocks.

Answering questions - you are able to personally answer any of the questions that your child may ask. Rather than having answers come from others (other parent, family members, etc.), you will be able to share and discuss the answers to their questions. You will be able to relate the circumstances and situation to them in a way that others will be not be able to. With instant feedback, through facial expressions or follow-up questions from them, you'll be able to ensure that their questions are answered clearly. You have a unique opportunity to discuss your situation - in a manner where you take personal responsibility for your situation and the associated problems it has created - thereby helping your child to decrease the chance for any possible feelings of responsibility and guilt. This will, once again help to remove potential emotional and developmental stumbling blocks.

Keeping the family connected - families should be viewed as complete units, consisting of parents, children and those other family members that play an active role in the overall family unit. The absence of one part of the family unit (you) can have a powerful impact on a families overall functioning. You can bridge some of that gap, which is created by your absence, by assuming an active role in maintaining communication with your child, especially through personal visits. While prison may limit some of the activities you can perform, you still can fill an important role in parenting your child. This requires that you play a vital role in knowing where they are at - emotionally and developmentally - and that you support their progress whenever possible. Where you cannot support them directly, you can play in active role, with their other family attachments, to ensure that any issues are addressed, any action plans for their well-being are developed, that progress is monitored and that positive encouragement be continually delivered to them. Communication is a must, not only with your child, but also with the rest of your family unit.

In some cases, a child may resist contact with an incarcerated parent. This resistance can arise from any number of separation trauma circumstances that the child may be experiencing, including: anger, fear, anxiety or worry. Barring any professional advice to the contrary, you should let your child know that you expect them to visit, or at least talk with you, periodically. Be empathetic and understanding and try to determine what feelings they are experiencing so that you, can help them to overcome these feelings. If your child's reaction to your visiting expectation is extreme, back off somewhat and try again in a week or two. Do not give up calling! Do not stop writing! Do not give up asking them to come visit! Work through any feelings of rejection that you might have and understand that this is more about how they are feeling and not how you are feeling.

Often times, the benefits of child visitation with you becomes a major topic of discussion, and a potential dispute, with the primary caregiver or other family members. Is prison visiting good for your child? Is the child visitation good for you? Is it good for the family as well? There is obviously no one right answer for every situation or family (a court or professional counselor may make a decision regarding this). If it is in the best interest of your child, they can benefit from the building and maintaining of family ties through the difficult time period created by your incarceration. Families need to communicate personally with their loved ones, even if they are in prison, in order to stay connected. Families also need to know how prisons and jails work, so that visits can go easily and with as little stress as possible.

Very often, it's hard for parents and a child to communicate, even without the difficulties that may arise from one of the parents being in prison. Teenagers and preteens, who seem to be able to talk with their friends endlessly, generally have a hard time talking with any parent for more than just a few minutes. The environment of a prison visiting room makes this task even more difficult. Getting conversations started or finding things to talk about can sometimes be challenging. These challenges can be overcome, by you, with some planning, preparation and perseverance.

Unfortunately for you and your child, the time and opportunity to talk during a personal visit is limited. You may feel pressure to make the conversation you have with your child count or you may want to make the time very meaningful for them. In this potentially stressful situation and environment, you may try and resort to asking lots of questions - questions that anyone, let alone a child, would find excessive and intrusive. Go easy, take it at their pace and try to listen more than you talk.

There are some important points to remember when planning for and having a visit with your child:

- the most important thing is that you truly listen to your child
- be focused on learning about how they're feeling and what is going on in their life
- the subject of what you actually talk about is sometimes less important than the fact that you are listening and caring for them
- a child may worry about telling you about "outside world" things for fear that it will upset you or that they'll feel guilty about having fun or that you are missing out. Tell them it's okay- you want to know what's going on in their life
- don't feel rejected when your child has little to say - keep a positive attitude
- the first visit is usually the most difficult - particularly if there has been a long separation. In this situation, it may help for

you to write your child a letter in advance telling them how much they are loved and missed and how much you are looking forward to seeing them. Especially with younger children, your letter can describe what you will be doing at the visit, what you will be wearing, any changes in your appearance, a description of the prison and visiting room and any other information that may make them feel more comfortable and at ease within this environment.

- don't be afraid to ask about what's going on in your child's life - not asking may make them feel that you don't care, are not interested or worried about what they may say

- takes things slowly - we all like our privacy - so does your child - they may want to reveal things about their life slowly - as they become more comfortable. They may be struggling with some big feelings - possibly ones caused by the current situation - trust and attachment takes time to build and maintain

- if you get a negative reaction, concerning your questions about their life or their privacy, back off to more neutral topics, like: weather, sports, school activities, family, music, etc. these things are still part of their everyday life and are safe for getting them to start opening up to you

- prepare for your visit - in addition to physically preparing for your child's visit (to minimize any delays and maximize the time spent with your child), you should also mentally prepare for the visit. Review your Parenting Plan, recent calls and letters, important dates and any other notes or material you may have. Set a few goals to accomplish during the visit, such as: telling your child you love them, affirming them, encouraging them, finding out how they really feel, finding out what's going on in school, what they're up to with their friends, etc.

Pre-Visit Preparation

It is important that a visit with your child go smoothly as possible. Visiting a prison is not an easy task due to the limitations, restrictions and the security processes that each facility employs. While some of the following areas may be very familiar to you, it's worth reviewing and possibly passing on to your child's caregiver or members of your family to ensure a "good as possible" experience for your child. Also, visiting regulations are frequently online and they should be reviewed prior to an initial visit.

Visiting list - at most facilities, anyone on an inmate's approved visitor list can visit. Each visitor must have a government issued photo ID. Children, usually, must be accompanied by an adult and if possible have identification. For caregivers, parental letters or copies of court documents may be needed. Each specific facility's rules may vary regarding the age where a child is required to have photo ID. Each specific facility's rules also vary on how many visitors may be allowed in at one time. Minors, not related to you and not accompanied by their parent, may need written permission from their parent in order to be allowed to visit. Make sure each visitor, or visiting group, has your inmate number.

Transportation – many county and city jails can be reached by public transportation. State and federal prisons are often located in remote areas. Some can be reached by public transportation, but may require several changes of trains and/or buses. In some cases a facility cannot be reached without a car and a taxi may be required. Transportation to and from the facility can be costly. In this event, ask other inmates or prison staff if any alternative services are available. There are a number of online blogs on the Internet where information sharing regarding transportation, hotels, etc. are available for each specific facility.

Visiting hours - each facility's rules vary regarding the day and time for visiting. Visiting hours information does not change that frequently, however, it is your responsibility to make sure that family members and caregivers are notified of any changes to visiting hours or if there is any possibility that you may not be there (court, transfer, etc.). Children can be heartbroken, worried and frightened if they travel to visit, only to find out that they will not be able to visit you. Tell your visitors to arrive early - there typically can be long waits between arrival at the facility and the actual visit.

Visiting type – each facility varies in the amount of contact allowed between inmate and visitor. Most state prisons allow visitors to sit together, move around the visiting room and touch each other. In other facilities, visitors are in the same space but are not allowed to touch. Still others allow minimal touching (hugs) at the beginning and end of visits only. The type of touching is monitored by the correctional staff. Many prisons do not allow contact. County jail visits are often through glass partitions with phones and others have video monitors and phones. Inform your visitors before hand, on your facility's policies regarding these matters, to avoid issues during the visit or even a termination of your visit. Setting the physical contact expectation of your child (especially younger ones) is of special importance.

Pre-visit searches - for each facility that provides in person visits, each visitor is searched. Corrections officials view visitors as their primary source for the introduction of contraband (primarily drugs and weapons) into their facility. Typically, the first search is conducted by walk-through metal detector (shoes and all metallic objects are scanned). If anything is detected on the person, the item (or items) must be identified and a determination made on its admissibility. If the item is undetectable, the visitor may be subjected to a hand scanner or pat search and may even be declined their visit. Some facilities have lockers and others do not. Recommend to your visitors that they travel light and be prepared to not be able to bring items into the facility (may cause delays arising from having to return to their car or hotel to store the non-permissible items). In the event your visitor has a medical condition (especially those with metal plates or screws in their body), advise them to always bring any medical documentation that will facilitate the search and admission process.

Allowable visiting room items – generally speaking, very few items may be brought into the visiting room. Depending on each specific facility's rules, the only exceptions typically relate to infant care (diapers, bottles, etc.) and these items are often held by the corrections staff until needed. Small amounts of money may be brought in for use in the visiting room vending machines. Advise your visitors of the maximum amount allowable. In addition, change machines are frequently out of order, so a good supply of quarters is recommended.

Visiting area - visiting areas vary greatly from facility to facility. Advise your visitors, especially your child, about the type of room and the chair/table set-up that they will be experiencing. Privacy is often an issue due to crowding, chair layout and surveillance requirements. Most facilities, unfortunately, offer few or no services/activities for children. Setting your child's expectations, and your preparations, regarding how you will spend your time with your child is very important. If your facility does have child or family friendly facilities, plan ahead and take full advantage of these services.

Visitor wear - each facility has specific rules regarding how visitors must dress, usually prohibiting athletic wear, athletic shorts, short shorts, revealing necklines, bare midriffs and backs, under-wire bras, sandals, and open toed shoes. Each facility may restrict the color of clothing and the types of sweatshirts, jackets, vests or sweaters that may be worn. On occasion, children may be given some leniency however, this is not always the case. Advise your visitors dress conservatively, especially on the first visit, until they are able to learn more about the specific facilities rules and practices. Advise your visitors that dress codes may be inconsistently enforced as different staff interpret or enforce rules in different ways. If there is a written dress code mail it to your visitors in advance. Advise your visitors to bring extra clothing, if possible. This will help avoid a canceled visit or the unexpected expense of having to purchase admissible clothing.

Visiting room food - each facility generally does not allow visitors to bring their own food into the visiting area. Advise your visitors about whether or not your visiting room has vending machines available. It is generally recommended that visitors not count on the vending machines as they may be out of order, out of supplies, or have generally unappealing items. In addition, the cost of the vending machine products are typically expensive. If possible, children and family members could eat before visiting, thereby avoiding missed visiting time while purchasing and preparing food, or having children spend an inordinate amount of time deciding, purchasing and or fussing about what they're going to eat.

Visiting room atmosphere - there are a number dynamics that typically are present in the visiting room and each can have an impact on your ability to have an effective visit with your child. First, there is an inherent friction between visitors and the correctional facility staff. Officers are present to maintain security and operate within a highly defined set of procedures. Correctional staff often see visitors as sources of contraband and as a disruption to the facility's regular routines. In many instances, unfortunately, visitors don't feel welcome and children are unable to realize the full benefit of the experience with their parent. Second, visiting rooms are often crowded, become quite noisy and frequently contain harsh language - especially during the busiest visiting hours. The ability to share personal matters, intimate feelings and sensitive issues, in a private setting, is frequently limited due to this type of environment and the close proximity of other inmates and their visitors. Notify your visitors, in advance, of the most child friendly locations to sit (typically near the front by the correctional staff). It may take a number of visits for children to overcome the challenges these situations present.

Visiting focus – all of your efforts, during your child's visit, should be focused on your child. Understandably (if you have a relationship to the adult bringing your child), there may a natural tendency to spend some time on family business or expressions of intimacy with your adult visitor. This is fine and natural, however those things that exclude your child or make them feel uncomfortable should be avoided. To maintain your relationship with your adult partner, you should try to schedule separate visits that do not include children. During these visits, you can engage in discussion of family business issues, discuss potentially contentious issues, have appropriate expressions of intimacy, and have conversations that your child does not need to hear.

Child preparation

One of the most important factors in a successful visit with your child is the establishment of their expectations regarding the visit. These expectations should encompass everything from the beginning of the trip, to check-in, to the visiting room and their return trip home. While some of these expectations can be set by you, they are typically provided by the other parent, caregiver or family member who is bringing them on the visit.

The preparation should start by informing the child of what they can expect the day of the visit. Describe how they will get to the facility, what it looks like and what the check-in process is like and how things will go during the security check. The more information they have and can anticipate, the greater amount of control the child will have over any feelings of anxiety they may experience.

The accompanying adult should help your child to identify and express their feelings, as well as offering them reassurance. They should attempt to ask them open-ended questions verses yes or no questions. This, hopefully, will open a line of communication between them and the child thereby allowing the child to verbalize their concerns prior to actually being confronted by them. This is an ideal time for the adult to help the child formulate questions for their parent. It is also a good time to focus the child's thoughts on specific things that they want to share with you.

Since visiting time is generally limited, helping your child to focus on several specific topics will help them to organize their thoughts more fully. The adult should assist the child in focusing on positive things that are going on in their lives, such as: school homework achievements, after-school activities, favorite movies, music, activities with friends, etc.

The role that the accompanying adult plays is very important. Children can be experiencing a wide range of emotions and their thoughts can be scattered. Often times, given their potential range of emotions, they will forget what they want to tell their parent, so rehearsal beforehand can play a very important role. The objective of the accompanying adult is to ensure a minimally stressful, quality, and more positive visit with you.

Specific, more age-related, preparation information follows:

Infants - younger infants like to be held a lot, look at things (especially faces) and they are beginning to respond to familiar voices and faces. As such and if possible, let younger infants hear a tape, video or phone call of your voice. The accompanying adult should also communicate with you, in advance, to let you know about your child's new and emerging skills (crawling, standing, rolling over, etc.). This may cause some initial sadness for you (arising from your missing out on important events), however, it will minimize any chances for distress that could arise during the visit.

Slightly older infants will be starting to crawl and move more, and like to make noises by banging and shaking things. They are beginning to make verbal noises (cry or yell), and may show a basic understanding of simple commands (waving, etc.). As such, any time prior to the visit should be spent where the child is unencumbered, minimal car seats, straps, and sitting. The accompanying adult should also communicate with you, in advance, to let them know what verbal skills and commands they have accomplished.

Infants may become cranky from the trip and the process required to get into the visiting room. They may become over stimulated and cry or simply may want to go to sleep. You should be prepared for each possible outcome.

Toddlers - toddlers are refining their motor skills with lots of walking, running and climbing. They are exploring a lot, imitating adults, testing limits and using their expanded verbal capacity. As such, be sure the toddler is well rested and fed - they are burning lots of energy. Do not give them lots of rules ahead of time - they won't remember them anyway with all the emotions and feelings they will be experiencing. Show them lots of pictures or videos of you prior to the visit.

Early childhood – these children are refining motor skills (drawing, etc.) and beginning to be more expressive of their feelings in words. Some are seeking attention, may interrupt frequently, may be seeking some control and will generally ask lots of questions about your daily life. The accompanying adult should read any letters, from you to the child, beforehand in order to focus their attention and memory on you. It may also be helpful to have them bring along (if allowable) any drawings that have been sent to them, by you, so they can talk about them during the visit. Prior to the actual visit, allow the child to have some control, power or choice over some things - this way they will be more willing to accept not having any control or power in the very restricted prison environment.

These children may also become cranky from the trip and the process required to get to the visiting room. As a result, they may express themselves and say that they want to return home. Over stimulation from all the activities may cause these children to exhibit hyperactive behavior or a feeling of fear and insecurity. Hyperactivity will make them difficult to control in the visiting room. Insecurity may cause them to become very clingy, to cry, or want to leave prematurely. Explanation of the process beforehand may help to alleviate the potential of fear and confusion.

Middle childhood - these children are very focused on their friends, activities and how other people feel towards them. They want to talk about their life, with you, but worry that they may make you feel bad if they talk about "outside" things. They may also hold back on their emotions so that the visit will go well.

As they are focused on their friends and activities, it may be difficult in getting them to agree to visit. They may be more verbal and ask not to come, ask to leave, make demands or become rebellious. Once there however, middle childhood children may find the prison and the security process kind of interesting and may you ask lots of questions about how the facility operates.

Adolescents – teenagers are exercising independence, control and expanding their relationships. As such, teenagers may resent having to make the trip and visit. The ride may provide them with an opportunity to dwell on any feelings of embarrassment or that they are missing out on other activities. Travel time may cause them to become angry, upset or withdrawn, so accompanying adults should plan activities or diversions for the journey. Teenagers are generally impatient and intolerant with the processes implemented by the prison. They may require time "to vent" at the beginning of the actual visit before they are able to start discussing things in their life or their feelings.

The Visit

As previously mentioned in this chapter, your objectives for a personal visit with your child are to: give you the opportunity to more closely relate with your child - express your love for them, see firsthand how they are growing and developing, see their body language and expressions, have physical contact (if permissible) and create experiences you both can draw upon at a later date.

The more prepared you are, the better the visit should go. Spend a short period of time, prior to the visit, mentally preparing: review your Parenting Plan, any recent calls and letters, and any important upcoming dates. Go into the visit with a plan and several goals. Especially important is that you tell your child that you love them, affirm their unique identity, encourage them and attempt to find out what's really going on in their life. Plan a couple of age appropriate activities - they can serve as icebreakers, create times of bonding or opportunities to just learn more about them.

What to talk about with your child during the visit can be challenging. Your child may require a few minutes to work through the feelings that have arisen from the trip, the security check-in and from the visiting room. Be prepared with some light conversation for the beginning of the visit, in order to give time them to start to feel more comfortable and to start opening up.

Your child may be tentative or afraid to tell you, in detail, about life on the outside as it may make them feel sad or guilty. You may be worried about sharing details regarding life on the inside, as you may feel it will scare them or that they may become bored. It is okay to talk about each of these things (with age appropriate discretion on your part), it is everyday life for both of you, and it is what both of you are missing and needing.

Encourage your child to discuss their feelings with you; both good feelings and bad feelings. They will be looking to you for understanding and guidance. It is critical that you be a good listener. You will also need to be patient and empathetic. This is a difficult situation for everyone involved. Just as you have good days and bad days, your child will also have good days and bad days. Not all visits are going to go well. A bad visit doesn't mean that your child doesn't love you or that you shouldn't have future visits.

Some facilities have child friendly areas with toys, games and books. If age appropriate, take advantage of these items. Find opportunities to praise them and encourage them during this time. Let them win the games. Take advantage of the opportunity to share in everything surrounding this time, such as taking turns, playing with toys, setting up games and reading time. Sharing things between you and them will create more connected experiences.

Specific, more age-related, visiting information and activities are as follows:

Infants - play games or find opportunities that include physical activity and contact (if allowable). Activities can include patty cake, playing peek-a-boo, counting with your fingers or theirs, playing the face game (happy, sad, etc.) and share the drawing of pictures (if allowable). Hold your child as much as possible (within facility policy and your child's level of tolerance), tell them you love them frequently and allow them to touch you often. When you're not holding your child, position them so they can see you. If appropriate, imitate the sounds they are able to make or even sing to them. For slightly older infants (and if an appropriate environment is available), let them move around or crawl or play active games with them. If your infant's initial reaction to you is one where they don't feel comfortable or react as though you are a stranger, don't push too hard, just continue to stay close to them. It may take several visits for them to start bonding with you. Some infants will bond quite quickly and become quite attached, even clingy. This is good, however, it may create a problem when it is time to leave. If this is the case, make your goodbyes quickly and don't try to trick them by sneaking way - this may cause trust issues with you the next time. Finally, learn as much as you can, from the accompanying adult, about where they are developmentally and what new things they are experiencing.

Early childhood - children in this age group enjoy games, physical activity, making silly noises and drawing. Make up short stories using their names as the main character. Recite poems and nursery rhymes. Have them practice their numbers and the alphabet. Read them a story. Talk about their favorite things and things you've shared together. Listen a lot. Tell them you love them a lot. As they are beginning to develop the basics of control and independence, giving them some choices (even little ones) is a good idea. Choices can include: where to sit, what to do, what to drink, what to eat, etc. As they are also exercising some independence, you should also give them some rules or limits; with consequences. Try to express rules in the positive – what they can do - and consequences in the negative. For example, "I would like you to walk over to the drinking fountain, if you run you will have to sit in the chair for five minutes".

Children in this age group can be very frustrating, no matter what environment they are in. Be patient, be understanding but don't be afraid to use discipline. Discipline is good parenting. You should prepare yourself for the potential of having a visit cut short if your child can not behave and follow your rules. While it seems unfair that you will miss out on time with them, it is important that they begin to understand the importance of rules and consequences (remember they are quite young so don't create unrealistic expectations and overly harsh consequences).

Answer your child's questions as best you can. Don't be afraid to talk about your daily life. Tell them you love them a lot, show pride in their accomplishments and listen closely when they speak about how they feel or what they are doing. Consideration should be given on how to end the visit as the time nears completion. It is much easier for early childhood children, to leave you, then for you to leave them (may create potential feelings of abandonment). So, if possible, they should leave just prior to the end of the visiting period while you are still there.

Late childhood - remember that children in this age group may have feelings of embarrassment regarding your incarceration and crime – so factor that into your approach. If possible give them a little time to adjust, once they arrive. Ask questions about school, their hobbies, sports, etc. Ask them open-ended questions, listen to their responses and stories they may have - don't ask too many questions or give them unsolicited advice - just listen.

Tell them that it makes you feel good when they talk about their life because you care about them and love them. Look for opportunities to have them tell you about their feelings. Pay attention for signs that they may be sad, disappointed, upset or angry. Let them know that you accept those feelings and want to talk about them- listen and be empathetic.

Talk honestly to them and about your life in prison. Answer questions as honestly as possible. Tell them about personal things regarding your life in prison - things they can relate to - like what TV shows you watch, books you are reading, classes you are taking or activities you are doing. Tell them that you love them frequently.

Teenagers - for early teenagers, spend the majority of your time just talking with them. Ask them what's going on in their life. Ask them about what is going on in school, with their friends, and what activities they're doing. Try to have open, honest back and forth communication. Ask them how they are feeling and what you can do to help support them - especially with issues at home. Listen and be empathetic. Tell them you love them frequently.

For later teenagers, ask about how they are doing in school and what their plans are for after they finish high school (college, work, etc.). Talk with them about their future plans for work, living on their own and other "real life" issues, like relationships, drugs/alcohol and any other relevant adult issues that you may be aware of. If possible, try to have your older teenager visit you alone so that the two of you will have time to talk privately. Listen carefully and be empathetic. Tell them that you love them a lot.

It is normal for children to have an emotional or behavioral reaction during or upon completion of the visit. This arises from the difficulty of reconnecting with you and then having to separate again. Don't take it personally. If your child is struggling during the visit and seems withdrawn or does not want to talk, don't push it too aggressively. You can continue the visit with the accompanying adult and talk about things that will create opportunities for your child to join in the conversation. Children struggling with these issues are not rejecting you - they are just having trouble managing their feelings. Be patient, it's a stressful time for all concerned. Try to be flexible and adaptable. In the event that a visit has to be cut short, tell your child that you love them and that you will see them again soon. You can call later or write a letter to them, telling them that you love them and when they are ready, you would like to talk about the feelings they were having. Be patient, it may take time for them to open up and share these feelings with you.

Ending the visit - let your child know about 15 minutes prior to the end of your visit. This will provide ample time to say goodbye and briefly discuss their next visit, any letters you'll be writing each other or any plans for things to be done between now and the next visit. It is also helpful to create some form of goodbye habit or ritual that the two of you can share and do together at the end of each visit, like singing a song together, a routine you go through, a special handshake, etc. This can help the child formalize the transition time (when they have to separate from you) and any habits you create can become a very reassuring factor to them. While your child may experience some trauma and be upset at the end of the visit, the overall benefits of visiting far outweighs these potential issues.

The end of the visit is a good time to emphasize how much you love them and how much you look forward to eventually coming home. You can acknowledge that you both may feel sad at the end of the visit but that this is normal given the situation. Once again, your child will find it is easier for you to leave first, rather than for them to be left while you go.

After the visit - the accompanying adult can discuss the visit and ask the child how they feel about having seen you. On occasion, children may become withdrawn and sad. This is a natural reaction, however, to them leaving their parent behind. The most important thing that the accompanying adult can do is to reassure them that: their parent loves them, that they are okay, and that they will be returning for another visit. Focus the post-visit discussion around the positive aspects of the visit and the things that they will be involved in - with you – in between the visits. If they are not ready to express their feelings, everyone concerned must be patient. It has probably been an emotionally and physically exhausting day for them. Often times, when given the space and support to feel sad and talk about their parent, the child will be able to "bounce back" much quicker, feel much better about their parental connection and appreciate the support that the accompanying adult provided.

It can be helpful if the accompanying adult asks the child about specific things about the visit, such as: what they remembered the most, what they liked best about the visit, what they didn't like, what they found hard to talk about, etc. This will give the child an opportunity to learn that it is okay to talk about their parent and it will also help prepare them for the next visit. This information should be passed along to you and you should factor it into your next visit preparation.

It is very important that accompanying adults separate their feelings about you and your crime, from the child's feelings.

If they don't, children can potentially withhold the expression of their own feelings - for fear of upsetting the adult. Typically in these types of situations, it may be necessary to seek professional guidance and counseling in order to support the child's overall emotional development in a healthy way.

You should consider following up the visit with a letter or phone call to thank your child for coming to visit and telling them how special it was to see them. You can also follow-up on the things that were discussed or planned to be done between visits. It is also a good opportunity to follow-up on specific activities, events, homework etc. Following up with your child is especially important in those situations where your child is unable, for whatever reason, to have regular visits with you. There are lots of activities (stories, games, puzzles, journals, etc.) that you can do to create interaction and connection points with your child during the time between visits.

While visits with you are extremely helpful in keeping your child connected to you, there are often behavioral reactions (increased anxiety or aggression) that may occur after a visit as they adapt or re-adapt to being separated from you.

These behaviors can be difficult or challenging and cause adults to reconsider their decision regarding visiting the incarcerated parent. Studies show, however, that most children better manage the trauma of parental incarceration and separation when they visit their parents.

It usually takes time for a child and their families to cope with all of the feelings that arise from a parent's incarceration.

While not visiting may appear to be easier on everyone's emotions in the short run, the "out of sight" and "out of mind" mentality does not work long term. Distance and the lack of connection creates lots of emotional confusion, unanswered questions, unfounded fears, and a rampant imagination for the child. While a child may have difficulty expressing these feelings verbally, they will typically and eventually show up in problem behaviors - at home, at school and in relationships. These will be harmful to your child over time.

- 5 -

Activities to Stay Connected

Your child needs to stay in contact and to be connected with you, while you're in prison, in order for your relationship to grow and develop in a meaningful way. Contact can be in the form of personal visits, phone calls, letters and other personalized activities.

Each of the contacts with your child, create opportunities for you to develop relationship connection points. These connection points give you the opportunity to show your child that you love them, care for them, are interested in their uniqueness, see how they are feeling and to learn about what issues they are struggling with. They will also help your child to adjust and heal from the trauma caused by your separation from them.

The value that each connection point brings to the relationship you have with your child is dependent on the quality and content of the interaction that occurs during the connection. As you effectively interact with your child, it will create an opportunity for them to potentially adjust their behavior and attitudes and to be more able to adapt to the new situation.

Interaction methods, goals and challenges were reviewed, in extensive detail, in the immediately prior chapter. Most of the points brought forward are also very relevant and important for use in preparing for and making phone calls and writing letters to your child. In fact, phone calls and letters should be viewed as extensions of a personal visit. As such, only several points will be made about phone calls and letters with the balance of the material being focused on activities that will give you an opportunity to connect to your child in a meaningful way.

Phone Calls and Letters

Phone calls from prison are typically very expensive and relatively short. In many instances, unfortunately, children are often not even included in a phone call except for a quick greeting and "How are you?" Understanding the financial limitations that are present in most situations, you should try to talk to your child as much as feasibly possible. Even if your time to speak with them is extremely short, resist the thought that the conversation is meaningless. With the appropriate preparation, you can make the time meaningful by following up on activities and issues that you have previously discussed with them. It shows you care, remember, and are concerned about them. In addition, their ability to even hear your voice, though it is for just a short time, may be more reassuring to them then you would think.

Mail from you is very important to your child and depending on the frequency of personal visits, it may be that most frequent type of connection point that you may have with your child. It is an opportunity to tell them how much you love them, to share information about what's going on with you, remember events (birthdays, holidays, etc.) and follow-up on outstanding activities and issues. Remember also, that a child gets very little mail, so mail from you will be a special event for them and they will start looking forward to it.

Understanding that prison is a negative and stressful environment, you need to focus on the fact that communication between you and your child should be positive. Before you call or write a letter, spend time preparing so that your will create a positive interaction with your child. Your ability to remain positive with your child will provide them with comfort, reassurance and hope; all important items in your child's overall emotional development.

Activities

Given the time limitations and frequency of personal visits and phone calls, you should initiate additional activities (to combine with your letter writing) in order to increase the number and quality of connection points that you have with your child. These activities will enable you to increase communication, create bonding opportunities, have fun together and provide memories that you can share with each other at a later time.

Activities will create an opportunity for you to remain actively involved in your child's life even though you are separated. Surprisingly, activities will create hope and provide emotional support for both you and your child.

A number of specific activity ideas are identified below with information about how they may be utilized. The activities are loosely listed in age order (starting with younger activities first), however, you should consider each, based upon the specific skills, likes and dislikes, temperament and personality of your child. Be creative, adapt each one so it makes a closer connection to your child and utilizes what access you have to any potentially required supplies. Most importantly, use the chance to build closeness with your child and have fun with them!

Drawing - children always enjoy receiving drawings and pictures. To increase interaction with your child, you can trace outlines of items and have your child color them in and send them back. You can also make a coloring book for them, by combining a number of pages with trace outlines of their favorite objects, shapes, hearts, cartoon characters, etc.

Mobile - you can use some of the drawings (colorful ones with hearts, etc.) that you have made, or the finished drawings from your child to make a mobile. Try to use words with the drawings (like I love you and their name). They may not be able to read them now but they will later. Depending on your access to supplies, someone at home may need to complete the final steps.

Placemat - using file folders or stiff paper(s) construct a placemat with drawings or pictures your child specifically likes. Also use their name, your name, love and praise words and lots of bright colors. You'll probably have to construct it in four pieces for mailing, and someone at home can tape or laminate it before presentation to your child.

Bookmark - very similar to placemat and with the same type of items on it. It's just smaller. Be creative, use recent events in your child's life (such as birthdays, grade advancements, sports, etc.). Encouraging scripture verses are also very helpful.

Make a hug - Trace outlines of your hands and arms (using several sheets of paper) and connect them with tape. Add as much detail as possible (fingernails, ring, watch, etc.). Write love messages or words of praise on the arms.

Calendar - make a calendar and mark off all the special events (birthdays, holidays, etc.) you know. Decorate each page with holiday specific (Valentine's day, etc.) or child specific (birthday cake) drawings. If you're out date is nearing, have the calendar run through that date.

Write a Poem -write a poem telling your child how special they are, that you love them, what makes them unique and what wonderful things they do. Use their name a lot or "You are" frequently, add lots of positive adjectives when describing them, and use lots of feelings or emotional words (happy, joy, glad, etc.).

Write a book – create short story about you, your child, your family or some fun or imaginary event. For younger children, draw lots of pictures and use easy words. Use a number of pages and add a bright cover with their name in the title and your name as the author.

Daily notes - write two or three dozen small notes, each expressing your love and a positive thought for the day. Mail them to your caregiver and have them give them to your child - one per day. Have them be creative - put them in a book, under their pillow, in their lunchbox, by their toothbrush, in the car, etc.

Love letters - you cannot tell your child, too much, that you love them. Write them a letter telling them the things that you love about them: the way they smile, the way they laugh, the way they care, the way they play, the way they sing, how strong they are, how smart they are, etc. Write love letters every two or three months, as they get older, you may want to adapt the things you say to be more age-appropriate and focused on recent things they've done in their life.

Special Stationary - have your child's caregiver or other family member send you fun bright, child oriented stationary. Use this stationary to write your letters to your child, it will help to make your letters stand out and will make your child feel special.

Share a story - start a story, the funnier the better, and mail it to your child. Have them add one or two paragraphs and mail it back to you. You add a paragraph or two and mail it back to them, and so on. Try to be very creative and encourage your child to use their imagination and have fun.

Pictures – if available at your facility, use photo tickets every few months and mail the photos to your child. As the saying goes, "A picture speaks 1000 words," so smile and project as positive an attitude as possible.

Holiday cards - use thicker paper or file folder paper to create holiday specific cards. And lots of drawings and personal messages to tell them how much you love them and miss them.

Cutouts - if you have access to newspapers and magazines, cut out relevant facts, pictures or articles that would be of interest to your child. You can send them along with letters, cards or drawings. Your child will appreciate that you know their interests and are actively seeking information to help them along in these areas.

Scrapbook – along with cutouts and if available, create pages of pictures, articles and information about things your child has a strong interest in. Caregivers can attain a binder or scrapbook for your child to add these pages to. Let your child be creative with "their scrapbook" and let them add anything from you they like: letters, drawings, stories, cards etc.

Awards - commemorate significant events (grades, graduations, sports wins, etc.) by creating an award for them. Awards will serve to encourage and praise your child and let them know how much you appreciate and love them. Awards can look like certificates or ribbons and are ideal for adding to their scrapbooks.

Question and Answer - especially in situations where personal visits and phone calls are limited, you can a develop question-and-answer time with them. On a separate sheet of paper, ask them a number of questions and leave room for their answers. If necessary, their caregiver can help them write or answer the questions and mail them back to you. This activity can work both ways, encourage them to write you with questions where you can mail back answers to them.

Lists - lists are a variation of question and answer, only easier, and are a great way to keep track of many of the little things that you miss by being away. On a separate sheet of paper, ask them to list things they like, dislike or are their favorites, such as: food, color, TV show, music, ice cream flavor, pizza topping, class at school, friends, etc. They will be happy to know that you have a genuine interest in them and their life. This is great information for you to know and will help you to more closely connect with them during each interaction opportunity. You can even make a copy of the same list and share with them what you like, dislike or what things are your favorites.

Puzzles - there are a wide variety of puzzles and games that you can play, with your child, through the mail. Simple games include word search, mazes and crossword puzzles. For word search and crossword puzzles, create a theme that is based on your child's interests (that you have learned from your **lists** or **question and answer**) information. Create puzzles that your child can complete during visiting date travels, that they can send back to you or just add to their scrapbook.

Bible Study - depending on the availability, you can utilize pre-prepared (age specific) material or create material on your own. Typically, several verses from popular Old Testament stories (Noah, Jonah, Joseph, etc.) can be written down along with several questions focused around the main principles of the story.

Childhood stories - children of all ages like to hear stories about themselves. Be specific as possible, giving ages and circumstances surrounding significant events in their life, like: what their first words were, when they learned to walk, what their first birthday was like, what toys they liked, etc.

Tongue twister - at the end of your letters or cards, create a funny tongue twister for them to try and repeat at home or during the next phone call with you.

Let's cook - if age-appropriate and an interest of your child, you can find and send home recipes that they can make under the supervision of their caregiver. There are many benefits to this activity, including: learning to cook, having a fun time, possibility of sending you some pictures of their food and the experience, and the creation of a memorable time that may stay with them for a very long time.

Magazines - if financially possible, purchase a magazine subscription for your child. The magazine subscription should be focused around one or more of their strong interests. The magazine will be a monthly reminder, of you to them, and show them that you understand their interests and are promoting them in a positive and encouraging way.

Sports - if your child is a sports fan, this is a great opportunity to share a common activity. Before a sports season begins, you can both pick your favorite teams and then follow them throughout the season. If available, you both can watch a specific game and discuss it later during a visit, phone call or letter.

I'm Going to Be - your child will have aspirations about what they want to be when they grow up. By taking an active interest in your child's dreams, you'll find a great way to increase the quality of your interaction and the strength of your connection to your child. Use some of the previously mentioned activities (magazines, scrapbook, cut out, share a story, write a book, etc.), in order to take an active role in developing and nurturing your child's hopes and dreams. Your honest interest in them will help them feel loved and cared for.

Positive Thoughts - with each letter, drawing, puzzle or other item you send your child, you have an opportunity to add a short item containing a positive thought or message. You can include a line or two from a poem, a quotation, a speech or Bible scripture. Positive thoughts can be focused around values, hope and encouragement or even something funny.

Goal Setting - spending time with your child, about their goals, shows them that you care about them and are interested in helping them to grow individually. Goals can be focused around any number of activities, including: developmental skills, behavior, school, sports, church, personal interests, chores, etc. Goal setting with your child allows you to get to know them better, show them your love and understanding and provide them with guidance and support.

Music - especially with older children and teenagers, music plays a large role in their activities. No matter what style, ask them to create a list of their favorite songs and send it to you.

If a portable radio available to you, listen for their favorite songs. Your child will appreciate your interest and you'll create an opportunity for sharing their taste in music. You can do the same, send them your list and have them listen for your music.

Friends - for older children and teenagers, friends generally are a critical part of their life. Take an interest in their friends and have your child tell you about them over the phone or in a letter. Follow-up with them in your letters. Your child's willingness to discuss their friends is important and can tell you about what type of personal choices, attitudes and behaviors they may be going through. The earlier you start this activity with your child, the easier it will be as they get older.

Sharing your spiritual journey - if you are developing your spirituality, you have an opportunity to share your journey with your child. The sharing of your faith and its principles can expose your child to the wonderful qualities of hope, love and compassion. The objective is not to preach to your child but to share the positive and hopeful outlook that faith brings.

Sharing Kindness - opportunities to be kind to others are often overlooked by your child and also by you (given your environment). Talk with your child and challenge each other to do one or two nice things for someone else. This activity will help each of you to grow your comfort zone, extend kindness to someone in need and learn how helping others really helps you both. Demonstrating selflessness to your child may prevent them from getting too wrapped up in themselves and their desires.

Life Lessons – for older children (especially older teenagers), you have an opportunity to share your life experience, good and bad, with them. Create a journal or series of letters and write down the things you are working on to improve your life. For negative situations, discuss how you are turning it into a learning experience and growing from the situation. The life lessons process may provide invaluable guidance to your child during a difficult situation and may prove to be extremely therapeutic for yourself.

Mentoring - depending on the attachment and support network available to your child, you may want to consider finding a volunteer to be a mentor to your child. A mentor can provide encouragement, support, unconditional love, life skills, and hope.

Working - for older teenagers especially, being involved with them regarding working is very important. Focus your letters and questions around their future work objectives and goals regarding their life. Knowing your child's life aspirations will help you to provide them with support, guidance and encouragement. Use the opportunity to develop your knowledge (with available magazines, library and other facility resources) regarding areas in which your child is interested.

Remember, your child needs to maintain healthy, constructive contact with you while you're away. Use these or other activities, on a consistent basis, so that you can develop a strong and lasting relationship with your child. Show them you are very interested in them and what they do; that you love them and will be there for them now and when you are reunited with them.

Dail-in number
(425) 436-6302
Free Conference phone
4MW-775

Access code
158144

Host Pin
1321

Made in the USA
Columbia, SC
09 January 2020